KEYS TO CROSS-EXAMINATION

Cody Herche

MONUMENT PUBLISHING
think, speak, persuade.

Keys to Cross-Examination

Published by
Monument Publishing
18725 Monument Hill Rd. Suite 13
Monument, CO 80132

Cover photography by Chris Jeub

Library of Congress Control Number:
ISBN: 978-1-936147-30-4

Manufactured in the United States of America
First Printing, January 2011

www.monumentpublishing.biz

"Cody has not only proven himself in the competitive arena by taking home the most coveted awards, but he has given back to the growing community of speakers and debaters with this most excellent book. Cody is truly 'training minds for action'."

- Chris Jeub, President of Training Minds Ministry, Author of Blue Book Primer

"Cody's reputation as a debater speaks for itself. Cross-examination is an overlooked skill in policy debate. Master cross-examination and set yourself apart. Cody's book is a well-researched, yet conversational, read filled with personal anecdotes. This book is brilliant. Both novice and varsity competitors will find it relevant. Take advantage of this opportunity to benefit from the experience of a seasoned debate veteran."

- Matthew Baker, 2008 NEDA Debate National Champion

"True to form, Cody is cogent, comprehensive and charming in his presentation of the critical skills and attitudes that will give students the competitive edge in cross-ex. I would heartily recommend this book to both Policy and Value debaters."

- Kim Anderson, Author of Coaching a Coach a Club

"Cross examination is the simultaneously the most important and the most neglected debate skill. In this book, Cody Herche opens up a vast field of opportunity for every debater who wishes to dominate their cross-examinations while maintaining credibility and likeability. It's an art and a science, both terrifying and exhilarating, and Cody has you covered every step of the way. Grab the Keys, and take control of your cross-examination."

- Sam Hoel, Team-Policy 2007 Hall of Fame Champion

"I cannot recommend this book enough for students and coaches of all levels. It brings together the best collection of cross-examination theory, tips, tricks and strategies that I have ever seen. Cody has always loved coaching and practicing cross-ex and that passion comes through in this book. You truly will not find a better guide to cross-examination."

- Shane Baumgardner, 3rd place team and 2nd place TP speaker; Extemp and two-time Impromptu Hall of Fame Champion

Contents in Brief

Contents in Detail

FOREWORD

By Vance Trefethen

Cross-examination is, in my opinion, the last skill that many really good policy debaters acquire. They may master affirmative case construction, come up with excellent negative analysis of tough affirmative cases, give powerful rebuttals, and yet still find themselves coming short of the goal because they don't yet know the keys to effective cross-examination. Cross-examination is really hard. But it's worth learning.

Treating cross-ex as more than just 3 minutes of prep-time for your partner and making it an integral part of the debate round will definitely improve your win/loss record. I have seen (and been in) debates won or lost on the basis of questions asked in CX. The right question can pry open a door that leads to victory.

But cross-ex is also a powerful life skill. Anyone who has ever been to a job interview has been in a cross-examination where the stakes were higher than any debate round. I am certain I have obtained jobs I would not have obtained had I not had the debate background where I learned to survive (and even enjoy) being cross-examined. There is a high demand in the world for people who can think and answer quickly and accurately under pressure.

Cody Herche has the analytical mind and the experience to more than qualify him to present to you *Keys to Cross-Examination*. Many of the techniques he describes here are techniques I've practiced for years in my debates with students and have taught them successfully in coaching sessions around the country. Cody not only knows them, he has practiced them and includes many practical examples showing how these techniques have worked in practice. His guidance will take you and your debate skills deeper and farther than you have been before, if you put them into practice. Open the door to better debating with *Keys to Cross-Examination*!

Introduction

I was twelve when I attended my first debate camp. At the end of a week of instruction, I found myself sitting next to Sam, a high school senior who graciously agreed to be my partner through my first team-policy debate round. Between my adolescent fingers I clutched four typed pages, a document Sam had written. The judge and timer were ready. I adjusted my clip-on tie and began reading. Six minutes later, my constructive was over, and I read the last words in the case. "I stand ready for cross-examination." I had no idea what that statement meant or the power and potential behind it. I had not understood much of my speech, but I knew that the next three minutes completely obliterated my case.

I sat down, shaken. It was early in the season and the examiner's questions were not well developed. But my responses were even more deficient. I was caught every time I tried to dodge a question. Each area of ignorance glared brightly. I had been so confident in Sam's case; now I did not know. I did not even know if I wanted to continue debating. The examiner had embarrassed me. I felt like my clumsy answers would never amount to much.

Sam nudged me from my reverie with the advice to listen to my opponent and write down questions for *my* cross-examination. A light came on in my head. I would get a chance to grill my opponent? I had just been burned, but a sizzling in my mind made me hungry to avenge my poor performance. With a twelve year-old's scrawl, I put my first crude cross-examination tree on paper and devoted the entire negative speech toward conniving ways to pin the speaker.

Sam assured me I did "great," but I am not sure. I am sure of this: those three minutes lit a spark that caught like wildfire. I understood that cross-examination -- the only time the judge is able to observe competitors speaking concurrently -- was an important element of academic debate. It was short, but it was the only time the debaters engaged in battle—the battle of credibility, rhetoric, persuasion and psychology. It was an incredibly important three minutes, arguably where debates are won or lost. I resolved then to improve my examination skills.

Since my initial introduction, I have witnessed over two thousand cross-examinations and have been privy to countless more Piranha Pack,

Conga Line and CX Tree drills. I have coached hundreds of debaters, many state and national champions, and plenty of novice beginners. I've worked summer camps, club meetings and tournaments. I've been an avid student of cross-examination through a decade of competition, always adjusting the debater's art. Today as a coach and law student, I still try to discover new strategies for a competitive edge for my students. This study has birthed a wealth of knowledge about successful cross-examination. In this book, I will share what I have learned.

Cross-examination is that integral part of a debate round when both the negative and the affirmative are standing before the judge defending their respective cases. Unlike regular speech time, cross-examination involves a simultaneous interplay of arguments between speakers as pointed questions are answered. A poor performance can doom an argument or an entire team; a good job can breathe new life into a point or otherwise assist in victory. More rounds are decided on a point made (or not made) in cross-examination than at any other time in the round. No speech impacts the judge more than the cross-examination. Effective cross-examination is therefore critical to debate success. Unfortunately, it is overlooked and treated lightly by many debaters. Unrealized potential is a hallmark of this pivotal period.

Most debate guides include a chapter on cross-examination. Some include strategic advice. But I have never seen a book that deals exclusively with this important debater's skill. When I competed, my coaches introduced me to authors like Robert Cialdini, Peter Brown, Francis Wellman and others. These authors wrote about the psychology of persuasion or courtroom cross-examination. These works are great works for lawyers, and their advice has so much cross-applicability to forensics. But the advice begs to be organized into a guide for debaters. *Keys to Cross-Examination* does just that.

It took me years to master cross-examination. I can honestly say that the cross-examination keys I acquired in my years of training led me to the final round of the 2006 National Tournament and helped carry me and my partner to victory. It also helped my attaining the top speaker award in Lincoln-Douglas debate the year prior. Ask most debaters how they learned cross-examination, and you'll get a hodge-podge answer. Most debaters make it up as they go along, just as I did for several years.

Keys to Cross-Examination pulls together the keys I profited from when I competed. These pages are full of keys that can be applied immediately to improve your cross-examination. The keys are written directly to you, the debater. They are short enough to be memorable yet long enough to be substantive. If you have competed for a few tournaments or have a rudimentary understanding of a debate round, I guarantee you will profit from this text.

I have four brothers, all of whom excelled at debate. As far back as I can remember, we have brainstormed cross-examination strategies. I remember late nights chatting with Ryan, my oldest brother and roommate, and my twin, Travis, who would sneak in for conversation. Even when talking about an unrelated topic, one of us would explore some new cross-examination strategy. "What if we tried to make the opponent think we're asking about topicality while we target the harms?" "I want to do a whole three minutes on one line of questioning." "I wonder what the impact of question tempo is on cross-examination?" Sometimes our ideas were zany, but some turned into great strategies that turned debate rounds in our favor.

Today we still toss ideas around and reminisce about cross-examinations gone by. Many of the tips in this book come from those brainstorming sessions with my brothers. Other keys are gleaned from legal strategy or reading trail advocacy guides. Still more are drawn from renown debate, psychology, law and persuasion experts. As much as possible, I have attributed ideas to their original source and provided citation information so that you can follow up and dive deeper. This text doesn't dive too deep into some of the complex theory like many of the ones I've studied. Instead, *Keys to Cross-Examination* aims to equip you, the debater, with strategies that will help bring you winning ballots.

Cross-examination is an art. It is difficult to master, just as difficult to coach, and nearly impossible to explain. Emery Buckner, a noted jurist and mentor to Supreme Court Justice Harlan, told the *Harvard Law Review,* "To ask a cross-examiner how he succeeds is to ask the artist 'how do you mix paints?'"[1]The constant references to cross-examination as art may induce debaters to believe that cross-examination is intuitive and that without careful preparation, they can rise to the occasion and wow

[1] Brown, Peter Megaree. (1987). *The Art of Questioning.* (Macmillan). p. 82

judges and other competitors. Cute anecdotes and TV programs notwithstanding, this is not necessarily true. As in other fields of art, some have unusual talents for their craft, but don't be fooled: a great deal of hard work is necessary for success. As Peter Megaree Brown said, "More cross-examinations are suicidal than homicidal." Because of the effort required for a debater to win consistently, I consider cross-examination to more than just an art; it is *a discipline*. Like art, cross-examination takes practice and experimentation, but it takes diligent hard work to become *great*.

There is little reason why a good debater--one who is willing to work hard, do the necessary practice and acquire the experience--cannot become proficient in cross-examination. No one can tell you what question to ask; cross-examination is impromptu, risky, anxious. This text will clarify the pitfalls and opportunities you will face when you take the podium. You'll face your opponent with credibility, skill and confidence, and you will win the exchange.

I have to smile when I think back to my first debate round a decade ago. All the theory in the world couldn't have helped me then. I certainly did not "peg," "prod" or "signpost" my routine. I doubt I "stuck to the Oracle" or "was the teacher." But I had then what you are demonstrating by holding this book: *gumption*. Like you, I was brave enough to start. My hope for you reading this book is that you profit from the keys contained herein and that you never lose your gumption. May these keys smooth your path toward forensics success.

Cody Herche

CHAPTER 1

The Ten Commandments of Cross-Examination

Cross-examination finds its most rigorous study in the field of law. Because a well-conducted cross-examination can make even the most persuasive testimony appear inaccurate, trial attorneys have strived for centuries to unravel the secrets of effective questioning. Accomplished attorneys devote substantial effort to studying the best ways of garnering revealing admissions.

My formal introduction into the lessons of cross-examination came at the hand of a local attorney. His son was a freshman in high school and was trying debate for the first time. Several students were practicing a Piranha Pack drill (where club members take turns firing off questions to one debater about their position) and I was on the hot seat answering questions about my case. I like to think I was doing pretty well. I had learned a few evasion tricks and was dodging some questions, particularly ones about the solvency of my case that might well have sunk it had I been forced to answer the examiner's queries in a more straight forward manner. The attorney watched our interaction for a few speakers before raising his hand and asking, "May I?"

> *Attorney: What is your understanding of the stock issue of solvency?*
>
> *Cody: It's whether or not the affirmative can guarantee that the harms will be eliminated.*
>
> *Attorney: Guarantee. [PAUSE] In one sentence, what is your plan doing?*

> *Cody: We are providing tax incentives to producers of alternative energy. Our goal is to-*
>
> *Attorney: Do you guarantee that the harms you cite will be eliminated?*
>
> *Cody: Well, we provide an incentive structure that will work to-*
>
> *Attorney: [REPEATING PREVIOUS QUESTION] Do you guarantee that the harm will be eliminated?*
>
> *Cody: We achieve solvency by providing an avenue for the reduction of the harm, but we can't necessarily guarantee an outcome.*

It took three questions for the attorney to get to the heart of the matter and only four for him to force me into a contradiction. In less than a minute he had dismantled my solvency and designed a line of questioning that everyone in club could use. I learned later that the examiner had employed a simple trick to help trap me (we will deconstruct the *Force a Trackback* routine in the *Examiner* chapter). But the attorney's confidence and poise during the exchange cemented my respect for him and the art of asking and answering tough questions.

After I graduated from high school and started college, the attorney offered me a job in his office working as a legal assistant. There, while preparing deposition and cross-examination questions, I learned that the goals of an attorney's cross-examination and those of a debater are very similar. Besides a few procedural changes, the only substantive differences are the three-minute limitation and the lack of an attendant lawyer to object on the behalf of the witness. In three years working in the law office and scouring the office bookshelves for texts on cross-examination, I found the keys to this art as well as a way to apply them to academic forensics.

Irving Younger

The late Irving Younger was a leading scholar on trial technique and advocacy. As a New York lawyer and federal prosecutor, Younger established a solid reputation as a skilled barrister. Throughout his 33-year career, Younger was best known for his sharp wit and theatrics in the courtroom. He had the rare ability to destroy an opponent's witness with a few quick questions.

Mr. Younger represented *The Washington Post* after it had been sued for libel by William Tavourlareas, the president of the Mobil Oil Corporation. A trucking executive was called to the stand by Mobil Oil. Younger delivered a cross-examination of only four questions:

> *Q: Mr. Hoffman, did you just get into Washington just about an hour ago?*
>
> *A: About an hour and a half, I would think.*
>
> *Q: Did you come up from Florida?*
>
> *A: No, I did not.*
>
> *Q: Where did you come from?*
>
> *A: Indianapolis.*
>
> *Q: How did you get from Indianapolis to Washington?*
>
> *A: On the Mobil corporate jet.*[2]

Younger later recalled that the exchange was a "hand grenade in the courtroom," the kind of moment that stays with a litigator for the rest of his life.

Far from hoarding the secrets to his trial success, Younger made a career of teaching young lawyers etiquette and strategy. Although Younger died of cancer the year I was born, he left behind the "10 Commandments" of cross-examination, which are heralded as the ultimate examiner rulebook and are, without doubt, the most quoted authority on cross-examination. This Decalogue provides debaters with an excellent introduction into the tactics required for effective cross-examinations. Forensics competitors should know them by rote.

---

[2] Labaton, Stephen. (March 15, 1988). "Irving Younger, Lawyer, 55, Dies; Judge, Law Professor and Author." New York Times.

1. BE BRIEF

2. SHORT QUESTIONS, PLAIN WORDS

3. ASK ONLY LEADING QUESTIONS

4. NEVER ASK A QUESTION TO WHICH YOU DO NOT ALREADY KNOW THE ANSWER

5. LISTEN TO THE ANSWER

6. DO NOT QUARREL WITH THE WITNESS

7. DO NOT PERMIT THE WITNESS TO EXPLAIN

8. DO NOT ASK THE WITNESS TO REPEAT WHAT HE SAID IN HIS SPEECH

9. AVOID ONE QUESTION TOO MANY

10. SAVE THE EXPLANATION FOR LATER

These commandments are keys. They are the building blocks of successful cross-examination which every lawyer must learn. They help the advocate toward his ultimate courtroom purpose: to persuade a judge or jury. In a debate round, you have an analogous goal. You are out to persuade. Champion debaters understand that successful cross-examinations are often the persuasive lynchpins of a debate round. Simply by applying Younger's decalogue to their current style, debaters can make a marked improvement in their persuasiveness.

If the only lesson you extract from this text is to adhere to this decalogue, the book will have been worth the effort. In later chapters, I will elucidate the justification for these rules and give examples from real cross-examinations. Elaboration will add perspicuity to the terse instructions above.

CHAPTER **2**

Critical Keys to Cross-Examination

"That reliability be assessed in a particular manner: by testing in the crucible of cross-examination." —Antonin Scalia, Associate Justice of the Supreme Court

You would think that a professional attorney has a harder job in front of them. They don't; you do. Cross-examination from a debater's perspective takes several more commandments—or «keys»—to gain a winning ballot. This chapter takes on the ones I have personally cultivated during my own years of competition as well as while coaching national champions.

Know Your Case

Your case is one of the few eminently predictable elements of the debate round. You wrote it, you researched it. The expectation is that you know it. If you do not know your case, deficiencies in knowledge will become apparent during cross-examination.

Demonstrated ignorance about a topic in which the judge expects you to be knowledgeable is poison. Would you buy equipment from a salesperson who did not know anything about his wares? If you had a choice, you would probably ask to see a different salesperson or perhaps leave the store. As a debater, you are selling a case. You should be a knowledgeable salesperson. Don't expect the judge to give much credence to your arguments when you fail to appear credible.

The year after I won the 2006 NCFCA National Tournament, I coached Sam Hoel and Allison McCarty, the team that took the 2007 title. My students were negative in the final debate round. The affirmative ran a case to abolish the North Atlantic Treaty Organization, or NATO, an organization that includes most of the countries in Western Europe. In the first cross-examination, Allison worked to set up an argument about France's reaction to the affirmative plan. Her first set-up question was, "Who is the president of France?" The affirmative did not know. Granted, the heavy lights were on, over 1,000 people were watching and the question does not concern an everyday conversational topic, but the affirmative looked ignorant not knowing who the French president was. Sam and Allison never made the affirmative's lack of knowledge a voting issue. They did not have too; the "I don't know" alone made the witness look unprepared.

Legal expert E. Barrett Prettyman Jr., who argued several times in front of the Supreme Court, reflected, "I am constantly amazed, during Supreme Court arguments, to hear an attorney virtually struck dumb by questions from the bench that anyone with any knowledge of the case should have anticipated. It is as if the attorney has become so imbued with the spirit of his cause that he has totally blinded himself to the legitimate concerns that someone else might have in adopting his position."[3]

Don't underestimate the importance of details, especially background facts. I was affirmative debating a change in trade policy with Niger, a country in West Africa. The round was going well until the second negative speaker read disadvantage evidence about how the people of Niger would react negatively to our proposed policy change. The evidence said that the Niger president, "Olusegun Obasanjo," was not amenable to American interests. The judges were attentive to the evidence and the disadvantage looked like it might carry the day for the negative. But something was not right. I knew that Obasanjo *was not the president of Niger*. I checked with my partner, who confirmed that the Niger president was Tandja Mamadou. I remembered reading that Mamadou had been in place since a military coup in the 1970s. After

---

[3] E. Barrett Prettyman Jr. (Winter, 1978). *Supreme Court Advocacy: Random Thoughts in a Day of Time Restrictions*. Litigation. 16, 18-19.

some reflection, I also figured out who Obasanjo was and stood up to cross-examine the second negative.

> *Q: May I see the evidence you read under disadvantage one?*
>
> *A: Sure, here.*
>
> *Q: Now it says here that President Obasanjo is not amenable to American interests, correct?*
>
> *A: Yes.*
>
> *Q: Who is Olusegun Obasanjo?*
>
> *A: I believe ... I think he is the president of Niger.*

That's when I noticed that there was more to the evidence than what the negative had read in the round, and that the next sentence supported my suspicions.

> *Q: Could you read the next line in the evidence, right after where you stopped in your speech?*
>
> *A: OK. "Obasanjo's calls for political reform are a welcome change in Nigeria, a country who's political landscape ..."*
>
> *Q: OK, thanks. Are Nigeria and Niger the same country?*
>
> *A: No.*

In 15 seconds, we destroyed the disadvantage and won the cross-examination. The judge was faced with two debaters, one of whom had confused Niger with Nigeria and another who knew the presidents of both countries. All three judges mentioned the exchange on their ballots.

There is no great trick to this. Your case must become your passion. You need to read as much background information about the topic as you can. When the resolution is announced, design a reading list around it and read assiduously during your summer break. If your case concerns a foreign country, read the CIA's *World Factbook* about that nation. If you are passing a bill in Congress, read the whole bill. If you are changing the tax code, learn who the experts are in that field. If you are quoting a philosopher to support your value, at least have read a quick biography about him online. Better yet, read his significant works.

For those pieces of evidence you use to support your case, print out the entire article of each main source and read through them on the way to tournaments. Make a habit of marking up those articles with your thoughts, or keep a pen and paper handy to write down ideas for later review. Don't just hope you'll remember; trust in your written notes. Think about your case by turning it over in your mind and regarding it from various perspectives. Brainstorm the weaknesses and imagine what you would ask as the examiner. Then prepare your responses for each of those weaknesses, even if you think no one would ever ask about them. If you are prepared for 100 different questions, you'll be set for the 20 your opponent chooses to ask.

Know Your Opponent's Case

If the negative team knows as much or more about the affirmative case than the affirmative team does, judges will take note. In policy debate, the expectation is that affirmatives are more apt to be knowledgeable about their case because they prepare it in advance and have the element of surprise. When negative debaters counter with unexpected knowledge, they can appear more credible than the speakers who are expected to be the experts.

In some cases, simply knowing the answer to every question is enough to head off potential arguments. My brother Jesse was negative debating against a case to prohibit the Environmental Protection Agency from regulating carbon dioxide (CO2) emissions. The examiner wanted to demonstrate that CO2 was the most common greenhouse gas. Jesse was asked:

> *What is the optimal amount of atmospheric CO2?*

Jesse responded:

> *The optimal concentration varies by expert, but it's generally around 300 parts per million, or PPM.*

The examiner was, I am sure, trying to illicit an "I don't know" that would hurt Jesse's credibility. No one in the audience really understood what the significance of the response was or how it would apply in the round, but we all understood that Jesse knew his stuff. The examiner was apparently satisfied with the answer because he moved on to another topic. The 300 PPM response was never referenced later, showing that the affirmative did not get what it wanted out of that question.

Establish Your Ethos

Greek philosopher Aristotle identified three modes of persuasion: ethos, pathos and logos. Logos, which is Greek for "word," means the internal consistency of a message, the logical clarity of the claim, and the effectiveness of its supporting evidence. We sometimes refer to logos as an argument's logical appeal. Pathos is Greek for "suffering" or "experience." It is generally associated with emotional appeal or garnering sympathy. Ethos is Greek for "character" and refers to the trustworthiness or credibility of a speaker. A speaker uses these three elements to demonstrate that his or her appeal is more valid than an opponent's.

Although all persuasive modes can be developed or detrimented in cross-examination, ethos is especially vulnerable. The question-response format makes sympathetic and logical appeals difficult, leaving credibility as the chief battleground.

The lesson of this key (and of the previous) is to work hard to gain credibility. Before ever asking your first cross-examination question, the more work you do to learn about your case and your opponent's, the easier cross-examination will be. Time spent educating yourself about the resolution is never wasted. You will be amazed at how often tidbits of information come in handy and minor topical trivia finds its way into the round.

You may find that judges are more willing to vote for the debater who appears smarter. The judge may not be persuaded by your argumentation, but if he is impressed by your understanding of the topic, he may chalk up his ambivalence to his lack of understanding and trust in your credibility. A passionate speaker who does not win the ethos battle looks like a loose cannon. The judge will observe this speaker like a curiosity, but not take him seriously. A logical presentation that falls apart on credibility grounds in cross-examination looks like hyper-intellectualism. Judges will disregard your analysis as highfalutin. During cross-examination,, you need be credible.

Beware the Criteria

In policy debate, a criterion is a weighing mechanism for the round. Debaters often introduce either policy-based propositions (i.e., reduce the national debt or promote general welfare) or a paradigmatic criterion (i.e., net benefits or stock issues) to aid the judge in evaluating the round. Whichever team best upholds its criterion deserves the judge's vote. Although debate can center over what the appropriate criterion should be, most rounds have at least some proposed weighing mechanism.

The key is to know where you are in relation to your criterion. If you know how the round is going to be evaluated, you can relate your questions back to the weighing mechanism or show how queries posed against you are irrelevant. You should feel free to point out any departures from the debate's parameters. Questions about arguments that don't impact the criterion are irrelevant. An aware witness can have the following exchange:

> *Q: Will your plan cost taxpayers more money?*
>
> *A: I don't think so, but that's really secondary in the context of the criterion. We should be focused on preserving human life first.*

Use expressions like, "In the context of our criterion that doesn't make much difference" or, "Given the round's weighing mechanism, we should be concerned first with ..."

As the examiner, be mindful of how your argumentation impacts the criterion and feel free to ask questions that challenge the weighing mechanism. You could follow up the exchange above with:

> *Q: So, you do not care how much it costs as long as you save a life?*
>
> *A: Yes, human life is priceless. It must be preserved at all costs.*
>
> *Q: If your plan costs $10 billion more and only saves one life, should the judge vote affirmative? How about $100 billion? $1 trillion?*

If you take this tack, you should introduce a more holistic criterion for the round as an alternative weighing mechanism. Provide the response to this cross-examination routine as a reason to prefer your criterion. If the witness sticks to her guns and refuses to back down at any dollar figure, use the criterion's inflexibility as a reason to oppose it.

Remember that the criterion is always open for debate but that it defines the direction of advocacy in the debate. If a question is irrelevant in the context of the applicable standard of decision, say so. If the standard is bad, ask a question that demonstrates its deficiency.

Short, Clear, Concise and Pithy

Athenian orator Demetrius of Phalerum once said that "length dissolves vehemence, and a more forceful effect is attained where much is said in a few words. ... Brevity is so useful in ... style that it is often more forceful not to say something."[4] That's good life advice, but Demetrius' words have special application for cross-examination: In an adversarial situation, your opponent will have no interest in clarifying your argumentation for the judge. It is up to you to be clear. Make clear speech a priority and always be concise.

Appeal to Common Sense

To persuade someone of a new viewpoint or position, you need to appear the reasonable advocate. Just as no one takes a raving lunatic with long, unwashed hair and crazy eyes seriously, so your judge will doubt arguments that are not grounded in common sense. Common sense is the shared ground in cross-examination. In its grip are the elements you're pretty sure the judge agrees with you on: We should not waste money, life has inherent value, justice is important, there ought to be some rule of law, etc. As another human being, your judge will have a sense of moral preference, tastes and feelings. If the judge believes that you share the same moorings, she will be more amenable to your argumentation. If the judge believes you disagree on basic common sense, your whole argument will be in jeopardy.

You can ask specific setup questions that appeal to a shared moral sense, such as:

> *Q: Is justice an important societal goal?*
>
> *Q: Should we waste money?*

---

[4] Demetrius of Phalerum. (1988). *Readings in Classical Rhetoric.* (Benson & Prosser). 256-258.

Q: Should governments enforce the rule of law?

If you're sure your judge agrees with you, any waffling on the part of your opponent will distinguish their "common sense" from the judge's. If your opponent gives the obvious answer, you can move quickly through your setup queries while establishing a rapport with the judge. These questions send this implicit—and valuable—message: "We agree on the basics, why can't we agree on my case?"

You can also make overt appeals to common sense. To introduce your reasonable responses, use phrases like, "I think that deep down we know we ought to" or, "At some fundamental level we all agree that there is an imperative." Your goal when answering reasonable questions is to include your judge in your answer, as if you are responding for both your team and your critic. Wash and cut your hair and tame your eyes by appealing to common sense.

Avoid Overt Emotional Appeals

Blatant appeals to sympathy or other emotions are generally regarded with suspicion and sometimes resented. Emotion is an important element of argumentation, but overt appeals are rarely taken seriously. Former federal judge Whitmann Knapp once wrote, "Every argument ... must be geared so as to appeal both to emotion and to the intellect. I think the basic difference between a competent advocate and a great one is that a competent advocate can only do one or the other, or thinks only one or the other is important. You get competent advocates who are very good in emotional cases, because they are adept in appealing to the emotion. You get competent advocates who are successful in cases that are on the dry side because they have the knack of appealing to the intellect. But a great advocate is one who can appeal to both and knows how to press the two appeals in such a way that one will not get in the way of the other."[5]

There is a difference between a blatant emotional appeal and a balanced appeal to the judge's sense of justice. Appealing to the judge's common sense or the thematic core is an integral part of persuasive argumentation. But beware introducing irrelevant facts or making an appeal that is too

---

[5] Knapp, Whitman. (1959). *Why Argue an Appeal? If So, How?* 14 Record. N.Y.C.B.A. 415, 417.

full of empty passion to be taken seriously. When in doubt, disguise your emotion with intellect. Phrase emotionally charged queries in the abstract instead of talking about specific examples. Use short, concise hypothetical questions instead of turning your case into a sob story. And if your judge doesn't appear to be taking one of your points seriously, quickly move on to the next question.

Identify Your Thematic Core

One of the biggest challenges debaters face is making their crazy ideas seem reasonable. My students and I come up with the zaniest ideas for cases. We have run cases to pull Amish buggies off county roads, legalize the ivory trade to protect endangered elephants, ship nuclear waste thousands of miles to a U.S. territory, and a dozen others. For each of these cases, we establish some principle that we think our judge will easily find persuasive. This principle, or thematic core, becomes a critical rhetorical element in our case and, as we'll see in the next key, an important tool for cross-examination.

How do you want the judge to describe your case after the round? What adjectives do you want him to use? When designing cases in our club, we bring in lay judges—friends, neighbors, parents, anyone who has an evening to spend watching and responding to a debate. After they watch the round, we conduct exit interviews to see what the judges retained. (We are more concerned with what they saw in the round than who they thought won.) We ask what they noticed, what they liked, what turned them off.

Invariably, the elements we stressed as our thematic core come up in these exit interviews. Judges don't remember how many people died in Darfur, they remember an impassioned plea for the rights of Sudanese victims. They rarely articulate the cost of our plan or where our funding would come from, but do remember the story of a cancer survivor. When we learn what judges care about, we understand what is persuasive. If teams debate well, generally the judge's first substantive comments after the round are about the thematic core.

What is your case's thematic core? It may be the thing that drew you to the idea in the first place. It may be the undergirding philosophy that supports your advocacy. Or it might be your criterion. Your thematic core is the persuasive thesis of your case. It is the one-sentence explanation about your case that you give to your neighbor when he asks where you go two weekends a month. It is what you want your judge to say after the round when describing your case. It is the essence of the persuasive power of your advocacy.

Here are some sample cases with accompanying thematic cores:

> *Abolish the death penalty—Absolute sanctity of human life/Uncertainty of capital crime verdicts render them arbitrary and unjust*
>
> *Allow Internet taxation—Rule of law and closing loopholes*
>
> *Abolish the Environmental Protection Agency—States' rights/Failure of government bureaucracy*
>
> *Legalize marijuana—Individual freedom/Eliminate lucrative black market*

Most judges are bound to agree that human life has some inherent value, that the rule of law is important, that states have rights under the constitution and that individuals have broad freedoms. They may not agree with you on the extent to which principles apply, but if you establish at least *some* common ground you can work from there to persuade the judge of your position.

Adhere to Your Thematic Core

Your thematic core should be ubiquitous in the debate round. The judge should comment to his friend after the round that you were arguing for "individual rights" not legalized marijuana. You were for human life not against capital punishment. Every speech should contain overtures to your thematic core, including cross-examination.

As you design your questions, feel free to use your thematic core the way you use common sense in your setup questions. Begin your line of questioning with an obvious restatement of your theme, perhaps by asking your opponent to affirm it. Then build your line of questioning from there.

I once ran a case to abandon plans to use Yucca Mountain, Nevada as a nuclear waste repository. One of our "harms" centered on the fact that the then-planned waste site was in the middle of an American Indian reservation and that proceeding as planned would violate a government treaty. In some iterations of the case, my theme was to "always keep our promises." The following exchange was common:

> *Q: Would you agree that as a nation we should try to keep our promises?*
>
> *A: Sure, we should make a good faith effort.*
>
> *Q: Well, do you agree that the constitution makes treaties the highest law of the land?*
>
> *A: Yes, you said something about that in your case.*
>
> *Q: But do you agree?*
>
> *A: Sure.*
>
> *Q: So promises are important?*
>
> *A: Sure, yes.*
>
> *Q: Have we made a treaty with the Western Shoshone Nation in Nevada?*
>
> *A: Yes.*

These questions simply reinforce the theme. You want to phrase them so that any effort by your opponent to waffle will be perceived as unreasonable. For example, you should not ask, "Do you think we should keep our promise with the Shoshone Nation?" Your opponent will simply regurgitate his disadvantages and harm responses. If you keep your questions about your theme general, you will give the witness no reasonable option but to agree.

Controlling Semantics

Are you pro-life or pro-choice? Do you support preventative war or are you antiwar? Are you fiscally conservative or compassionately responsible? The words we use to describe our political views reveal a lot about what those views are. Semantic differences frame our debates' forensics as much as in real life. And disputational semantics often evidence substantive differences between sides.

I was negative debating a practice round against a couple of students about the environmental topic I mentioned earlier. The affirmative case revolved around the "endangerment finding" by the EPA which found that CO2 was a pollutant. My partner and I decided before the round that we would call this finding a "memo" throughout the round in order to trivialize its importance. We wanted the judge to think it was insignificant and that any change would not produce noticeable advantages. In the first cross-examination, I asked to see a copy of the "EPA memo." My student did not correct me and the semantic debate was on. When the second affirmative speaker referred to the endangerment finding as a "memo," my partner and I bumped fists; we had gained control of the semantic debate.

You need to control the semantics. Decide what to call important terms and how to pronounce key names. Will you use the acronym or say the whole phrase? Will you emphasize the second or third syllable? Gently correct mistakes in cross-examination ("Did you mean the "endangerment *finding?*"), incorporate the accurate pronunciation in your speeches and do not let your opponent push you off your semantic game.

Even "meaningless" differences can be significant. When my partner and I ran a case to amend the Employee Retirement Income Security Act of 1974, our opponents started calling the act the E-R-I-S-A instead of pronouncing the acronym like a word. We foolishly followed suit, adopting their style of reference and spelling out the act. Although the judge never mentioned the semantic discussion on the ballot, the shift in control was apparent to everyone in the room. We lost that round, in no small part to the ability of our opponents to win the semantic debate. Thereafter, we corrected any opponent who "mispronounced" ERISA and kept control of the semantic debate.

Power Semantics—Positive and Negative

Mississippi judge James Robertson recounts some excellent examples of disputational semantics in his article "Reality on Appeal." He recounts one example from when he was in private practice and was challenging "outside speaker" regulations at the University of Mississippi. Robertson argued that the regulations were too restrictive and sought to have them removed. During the court proceedings, he referred to the lawsuit as the "speaker-ban case." Soon everyone was doing it. That done, Robertson says, the outcome of the case was foreordained. Who could vote for a speaker ban?[6]

Words are not just defensive. If you can think of a way to rephrase an element of your opponent's case so it sounds better for you, do so! Introduce the shift in cross-examination, by asking a basic question that incorporates the new term. For example:

> *Q: The EPA memo was filed last April, correct?*
>
> *Q: Has the E-R-I-S-A been challenged in court?*

If you can land your semantic jab in cross-examination, you will have a much easier time incorporating the shift in your speech.

If a bill you are arguing for contains some good buzz words, don't refer to it by its acronym. For instance, a team advocating the expansion of the Freedom of Information Act would be foolhardy to call the act by its stolid acronym FOIA. Brainstorm catchy ways of referencing your plan action. Say "the Business Should Mind Its Own Business Act" instead of "H.R. 4431." As you think, write down the ideas you come up with. Remember that a brainstorm is worth little if the storm never leaves your brain to wreak havoc in a debate round.

Use this same tool on your opponent's taglines. If her first harm was "Economic Collapse and Devastation," refer to it as the "First Harm," "Economic Argument" or "Economic Harm." Don't keep saying "Collapse and Devastation" simply because your opponent did. Power up your semantic skills and turn the language around.

Be the Teacher

A bright spring morning several years ago, I was doing a Piranha Pack exercise with my club (see chapter "Cross-Examination Drills" for more on Piranha Packs). I stood at a music stand while my clubmate cross-examined me. The rules of Piranha Pack put little or no time limitation on the examiner and I was starting to sweat as my opponent grilled me. The longer the examination continued the more defensive I became, until the

---

[6] Robertson, James L. (1992). *Reality on Appeal. Appellate Practice Manual.* (Priscilla Anne Schwab). 119, 124-125.

examiner could virtually stand still and watch the credibility pour out of me. I had become so scared of offering an admission that I spoke and acted in a way that informed the entire audience of my fear. My anxiousness evidenced itself in evasiveness as I sidestepped question after question like an action hero dodging punches. Few of the hits landed, but they didn't have to. I was destroying my credibility just fine all on my own.

My breakdown was symptomatic of a bad mindset. Instead of trying to supply answers in a helpful way, I was treating cross-examination as a time to cover my backside. I was shielding myself at every turn. I didn't want my opponent discovering my case's weakness, so I headed down irrelevant rabbit trials, evaded questions and generally avoided answering his questions. I was also looking nervous and shifty, two things the members of the audience identified later as a detraction from my overall presentation.

In trying to correct that examination, one of the parents in our club came up with the admonition to "be the teacher," and it has since helped my cross-examination immeasurably. The concept is simple: Act like an instructor while answering and asking questions.

Teachers have some of the most natural credibility in society. Their occupation is to impart what they know to others and they are therefore widely believed and rarely questioned. Teachers are sought out for information on a host of issues, and their perspective is almost universally respected. A student who questions his teacher rudely, irrelevantly or even excessively is acting in contempt of a socially acceptable standard of tutor-pupil relations. This is the kind of student who, in the old days, was sent to the corner with a dunce cap and is now told to run extra laps during PE.

In the classroom, a teacher's word is gold. *Your* word should be gold in the debate room. When the examiner asks you a question, think of your little sibling asking you to help him with his math homework or your Sunday School students asking about the lesson. Think of the demeanor any of your teachers have assumed when answering a question and try to emulate their poise. You should be understanding of their confusion, but never hesitate in providing the answer. You should give them the information they've requested and anything else they want to help them along.

If the examiner tries to cut you off, be a little surprised at the interruption, but remember that you are there to help the student and listen kindly as the next question is asked. If the examiner is looking for a word or struggling to think of a country's premier, politely provide the correct data. If the examiner seems lost or can't find his place in a question, offer some direction—toward a question you are prepared to handle, of course.

A change of mindset did a world of good for my cross-examination. Instead of being threatened and retreating from questions, I worked to "help" my "student" get the answer they wanted. I became more focused on explaining than dodging. I consider that afternoon a turning point in my cross-examination ability. If you work on it, you should be able to be the teacher through even the toughest Piranha Pack.

The Judge Is a Respected Intellectual Equal

The solicitor general of the United States—the most frequent advocate before the Supreme Court—is sometimes called the "10th justice" because of the respect with which he is regarded by the members of the high bench.[7] This is the kind of relationship you want to foster with your judge—a relationship of respectful intellectual equality.

When you present in cross-examination, you want to have this relationship firmly in mind. It is *not* the relationship of teacher to student that you show to your examiner. And it should never express itself as paternalism. Judges who get the impression you are talking down to them will be turned off by your content or, worse, be antagonized by your attitude. You are not there to cajole favor from the judge or to bully him. Your presence is as an experienced, though junior member of a business team explaining something to the boss. You respect your boss's authority and general knowledge, but you feel confident in the area being discussed. So your attitude should demonstrate an acknowledgement of the judge's authority while exhibiting self-assurance in your own understanding.

---

[7] Scalia, Antonin and Garner, Bryan A. (2008). *Making Your Case: The Art of Persuading Judges.* (St. Paul, MN: Thompson/West). p. 33.

Canadian lawyer T.W. Wakeling once said that "an advocate should be instructive without being condescending, respectful without being obsequious, and forceful without being obnoxious."[8] Few judges want to be told how to vote and fewer still want to be begged. Judges want to be advised by an intellectual equal they can respect. They want a credible advocate to guide them reasonably to a decision. Adhere to these ideas and your judge will be receptive to your words and amenable to persuasion.

Restrain Emotion

Early in my freshman year, while my brother Travis and I were first cutting our teeth on academic debate, I observed a brilliant cross-examination. Travis had just finished a hard-hitting constructive and was ready for questions. It was apparent from the examiner's manner that something about Travis' presentation had upset him and it did not take long once the cross-examination started for the examiner's emotions to get the better of him. His voice rose, his questions became terse and mean, and he generally demonstrated his lack of emotional control. My vantage point at the table denied me a good look at the exchange, but friends in the room recounted afterward that the examiner's face became red and his eyes were bulging in anger.

What made this a brilliant cross-examination was Travis' restraint. During the angry barrage of questions, he maintained a cool appearance. He answered questions calmly and without the slightest hint of discomfort. He never looked at his examiner even when the examiner turned and asked questions directly to Travis. Travis' attitude not only kept the cross-examination from devolving further, it made the examiner more angry, escalating his passion until he had lost all credibility.

Judge Learned Hand, who was appointed to the federal bench by President William Howard Taft in 1909, advised young lawyers that "it is all right for you once in a while to *act* indignant, but never *be* indignant."[9]

---

[8] Wakeling, T.W. (1979). *The Oral Component of Appellate Work.* 5 Dalhousie Law Journal 584. p. 590.

[9] Poytner, Dan. (2004). *The Expert Witness Handbook, Revised 3rd Edition: Tips and Techniques for the Litigation Consultant.* Para Publishing. p. 150.

Author and barrister John Clifford Mortimer said, "The secret of cross-examination is not to examine crossly."[10]

Ideally, you should invoke rather than display indignation. Travis' controlled emotions were a stark contrast to the examiner's out-of-control tirade. His ability to endure the fire earned him excellent speaker points and us a win. When you debate, then, cultivate a tone of civility. You want to show that you are not blinded by passion and that your reason always dominates your emotion.

Do Not Accuse

Part of cultivating a tone of civility is never accusing other debaters of bad faith or trickery. Even if you have evidence that the other side is doing something underhanded, your public presumption should always be that your opponent has misspoken or erred inadvertently. Never accuse her of deliberately trying to mislead the judge or misrepresent information. Louisiana district judge Morey Sear said, "An attack on [the opposition] undercuts the persuasive force of any ... argument. The practice is uncalled for, unpleasant, and ineffective."[11]

If your debate career extends for any great length of time, you *will* observe both chicanery and mean tricks. Often, the fact that an author has been misquoted or a fact misrepresented will be revealed in cross-examination, since that is the time when suspicious areas are explored. And it is in this arena where champion debaters are most distinguished from petty ones—by how they handle their opponents' inappropriate behavior. A skilled advocate maintains his calm composure and assumes (at least outwardly) that the mistake was honest. The experienced debater treats the situation the way a teacher would handle a pupil who had just erred—by providing gentle correction without judgment.

Your judge will be able to see if there has been foul play by observing the round and inspecting the evidence. If there has been unethical behavior,

---

[10] Mortimer, Clifford. (2008). *Traffic Safety News*. p. 8.

[11] Sear, Morey L. (1995). *Briefing in the United States District Court for the Eastern District of Louisiana.* 70 Tul. L. Rev. 207. p. 224.

the judge will be impressed by your composure and unwillingness to lower yourself to trivial accusations.

If after the round you're still convinced your opponent purposely cheated, explain the situation to your coach and leave the problem there. Your coach will either contact the other debater's coach and the tournament director or will leave the matter alone. Your obligation is to maintain your class and stay above the fray by not making accusations or taking cheap shots. Once you have confided in your coach, the matter is out of your hands. Relax and go on to the next round.

Strengthen Your Command of the Spoken Word

Former British judge Lord Birkett once said, "Cultivate the love of words. It is important to cultivate words, to select the right words, to put them in the right order, to know something of their association, of their sound."[12] You would have no confidence in a carpenter whose tools were dull and rusty or a doctor whose scalpel needed sharpening. As a speaker, the tool you use to convey your thoughts is the spoken word. You must acquire and hone the most effective version of that tool available.

Eloquence is expected during speeches—especially prepared ones like the 1AC—but it is rarely demanded in cross-examination and its appearance is a welcome surprise. Speakers often demonstrate amazing rhetorical skill and astounding prose during their speeches, only to become listless and automatic in cross-examination. But if anything it is *more* important in cross-examination for your words to be precise and your grammar accurate. When exchanges become more impromptu, those with a good command of the spoken word are clearly differentiated from who don't have it.

Of course, improving your command of spoken English is not something you can undertake the week before a tournament. It is a lifelong project that you will revisit continuously. Fortunately, it is also a pleasant project, largely because the first step is to read good literature.

---

[12] Dolin, Kieran. (2007). *A Critical Introduction to Law and Literature*. Cambridge University Press. p. 25.

I have found that my speaking and writing style emulates the author I am currently reading. When I read Western novelist Louis L'Amour, I talk like a cowboy. When I read classic British author Charles Dickens, I use words like "humbug" and "fusty." If you read nothing but cheap novels, you will speak like the characters in those books. Develop a habit of good recreational reading. If you read well-written prose for fun, your everyday speech patterns will change for the better.

Next: Learn to write. If you have ever heard a best-selling author give a lecture, you will realize that good writers generally make good speakers. So start writing. The author who rarely puts pen to paper (or fingers to keyboard) will not write well. Look for opportunities to write—student essay contests, letters to friends, daily journal entries, etc.—that will force you to spend more time crafting prose. You will find that words come to you more easily if you are writing regularly.

Develop a vocabulary list with words you want to incorporate into everyday language. Learn what *castigate*, *denouement* and *juxtapose* mean and use them in sentences. Add a new word daily and try to mix it into at least one conversation.

As you expand your vocabulary, you can greatly improve your command of English by consulting books on grammar and usage. Try Patricia O'Conner's *Woe Is I* (Riverhead Trade, 1998) or Norman Lewis' *Thirty Days to Better English* (Signet, 1985). These titles may at first seem intimidating to all but the most ardent language fanatic, but are actually quite engaging once you get started.

Veteran trademark lawyer Leonard Michael tells a story about a talk he went to by the German sociologist Jürgen Habermas. Afterward, a young woman in the lecture hall raised her hand and said, "I'd like to ask a question, but I'm not into words."[13] Get into words. If you are able to present well considered prose in cross-examination, you will differentiate yourself from those who let their speech slide when they finish their constructive.

---

[13] Brown, Peter Megargee. (1988). *The Art of Questioning: Thirty Maxims of Cross-Examination.* Wiley. p. 53-54.

Clarity Is King

When you present in cross-examination, the first goal of your communication is to be clear. This feature of good style trumps all others, including literary elegance, erudition and sophistication of expression. If, for example, a vocabulary word might confuse your judge and render your statement incomprehensible or a particular expression has two meanings, choose the option that provides the most clarity.

If a question is unclear, the admission garnered will suffer from similar ambiguity. Your judge might not follow the response because the query was too complicated or verbose. Do not let eloquent phrasing detract from the overall goal of clarity. Judge Irving R. Kaufman put it best when he said, "All the careful strategy in the world will be of no assistance to you unless you [communicate] clearly and forcefully. And clarity and power are above all the fruit of simplicity."[14]

Banish Jargon

Jargon is any word or phrase that is used almost exclusively by debaters or experts in the debate topic. These words are typically employed in place of plain-English terms that express the same thought. When jargon is the only way to communicate a precise meaning and you are *sure your judge will follow*, you may allow yourself to use a term or two. But stringing together several linked jargon terms or using debate-specific verbiage when a more universal English word will suffice is unacceptable.

I watched a round where the affirmative advocated reforming fishery standards to make aquaculture more sustainable. The negative debater jumped into cross-examination with a question about "MSC Principles." Instead of clarifying for the audience what these principles where and what bearing they had on the round, the affirmative speaker tossed in some acronyms — NOAA, NWFSC and FDA. By the third question, the cross-examination was flooded with terms that floated around like so much flotsom. No one could keep up. Any admission earned by the

---

[14] Kaufman, Irving R. (1978). *Appellate Advocacy in the Federal Courts.* 79 F.R.D. 165. p. 169.

negative's efforts was severely tainted by the confusion caused by the jargon infusion.

Do not say, "Your position is para-metricizing the round so the ground is unfairly distributed." Say instead, "Your interpretation of the topic doesn't make for a fair and even debate." Rather than "This is not a prima facie case," say "Even if we accept every contention from the other side, they have not proven their position." Unless you are certain your judge will follow your explanation of the stock issues, be sure to provide some explanation before you use them regularly.

Use Acronyms Wisely

Acronyms are mainly employed as a convenience for speakers, shortening long phrases and titles into more "manageable" mouthfuls. For an audience, however, they can muddle the discussion by forming a confusing mesh of unfamiliar letters. And without clarification, acronyms do nothing to guide your judge.

Feel free to use commonly known acronyms (FBI, EPA, NASA), and especially so when referring to organizations that are best known by their initials ("FEMA" instead of "Federal Emergency Management Agency"). Your judge will probably be familiar with these acronyms, so you should feel no compunction about employing them.

Often debaters will design cases around an acronym. If the affirmative plan is passing the Firearm Licensing and Record of Sale Act of 2009 (H.R. 45), they might use the acronym "FLRS Act." They use a shortened term to avoid the necessity of saying the entire—very cumbersome—bill title every time they reference the act. Although the judge and opposing team might have no idea what the FLRS Act is, they'll become acquainted with the term and the bill over the course of the round if the debater is careful to link the acronym to its source two or three times.

When asking questions about an organization for which your opponent has given an acronym, be cautious. You do not want to start talking about the FLRS Act until the judge fully understands that you are referencing the affirmative team's plan. It's a simple thing, really, but it often trips up debaters. The key is to target the acronym early with a setup question that lets everyone know what the acronym means:

> *Q: The FLRS Act—that's the bill the affirmative is passing, correct?*
>
> *A: Yes.*
>
> *You can then ask questions about the act knowing that the judge is on the same page.*
>
> *As the witness, you need to be mindful of the acronyms employed by the examiner. When presented with an acronym that is off the beaten path, even if you know what the acronym means, ask for clarification:*
>
> *Q: Was the FLRS Act sponsored by Blair Holt?*
>
> *A: When you say FLRS Act, you mean the Firearm Licensing and Record of Sale Act, right?*
>
> *Q: Yes.*
>
> *A: Yes, the FLRS Act was sponsored by Holt.*

Even if the acronym was originally introduced by you, it does not hurt to refresh your judge's memory. Incorporate the full title into your first cross-examination response and reintroduce the acronym at intervals.

Acronyms, then, are much like debate jargon: a necessary evil that should be handled with caution and as much clarity as possible. They are great ways of saving time while speaking, but you don't want to lose your judge with one that's poorly explained.

Master Pronunciation

When I wrote a case about regulation of genetically modified foods, my opening line emphasized that these foods were integral to our food supply. But I never bothered to look up the pronunciation of *integral* and ended up erroneously putting the emphasis on the second syllable ("inTEgral"). A judge commented that she had a hard time taking me seriously after my comic mispronunciation. She mentioned the mistake twice on the ballot and voted negative. Since that round, I have heard debaters mispronounce many words they should know—words such as "subsequent," "candidate" and "nuclear."

You want to convince the judge that you are an expert speaker. And someone who mispronounces common words will never be taken for an expert. Besides avoiding slang ("ain't") and other informal words ("yep"), using accurate pronunciation is the best way to maintain the appearance of English proficiency. Ensure that your pronunciation of proper names, case-specific terminology and even everyday words is orthodox. Common mistakes include pronouncing *athlete* and *realtor* as though they were three syllable words and adding an extra *u* to the middle of *nuclear*.

When in doubt, consult a dictionary. *Dictionary.com* has a built-in pronunciation tool that is very helpful. To proactively prepare yourself, pick up Charles Harington Elster's *Big Book of Beastly Mispronunciations: The Complete Opinionated Guide for the Careful Speaker* (Mariner Books, 1999). Elster's entertaining essays provide the best ways to say the toughest words in the English language.

First Names

We are programmed from an early age to pay attention when people use our first name. When we were young and we disobeyed a parent's directive or were about to stumble into danger, someone would say our name to stop us. As we grew older, our name became our individual moniker. When someone said our name, they were directing their comments exclusively to us. Our training tells us to pay attention for our own safety and out of reverence for the title. Even in a crowded room full of chatting people, we will lift our heads if someone says our name. Someone is talking to us and we know we should listen.

As a witness, using your opponent's name demonstrates the effort you are making to tailor your response to meet the demands of the examiner. It helps to reset the question and give you an opportunity to answer the question in a more personal fashion. Saying, "I think I understand your question, Cody, let me see if I can answer it satisfactorily," or, "Sure, Cody, let me get that for you," brings you to the same level as your examiner. It acknowledges the question while keeping your opponent from interrupting. You just said their name and are about to answer their question directly—how can they interrupt you now?

When you ask questions, use your opponent's name to stop him from rambling. I find that I often pull up and stop speaking if someone uses my name. After all, it's what I've been trained to do since Day One. If a question has been answered and the witness continues to speak, say something like, "Thanks, Cody. My next question is ...," or, "Sure, but

Cody can you tell me ..." Using your opponent's name as the examiner is like pulling the reins on a horse. It will shift the conversation's direction back to you and allow you to continue leading the cross-examination.

First names are more personal than last name references. I advise against using only last names since most people do not inherently identify with their family name. I don't stop when I hear "Mr. Herche," but I pause when someone calls "Cody." Remember that you are your opponent's equal. Showing deference through a formal title is not necessary. You should refer to your judge with a respectful title, but talk to your opponent the way you would a peer.

I will note here that a minority of judges feels first name references are too informal for academic debate and therefore inappropriate. If you know who these judges are, adjust your first-name references accordingly. But the general rule is that it is best to use first names, in part because referring to other debaters by their first names helps the judge keep the speakers straight. With four debaters standing up and sitting down in quick succession, identities can become confused. Name dropping keeps the judge abreast of who is doing the presenting and can help the judge feel more comfortable with the progression of the round.

Organize Material for Easy Retrieval

Whether asking or answering questions, you are always trying to be in control of the cross-examination. One of the best ways to *lose* control is to be disorganized. Most cross-examinations contain at least a few seconds of fumbling papers and frantic searching. The witness is looking for the evidence she read in her speech. The examiner is hunting down his next question. It's on a Post-it note somewhere!

Pauses are an integral part of cross-examination and communication in general. But like a visit from the in-laws, they are always better planned. If you just presented material during your speech, it should be organized for easy retrieval. If you just asked a question, your follow up or the start of your next line should be within your sight. Fumbling papers only creates an embarrassing silence. Organization allows you to avoid this pitfall.

You Are Always Being Watched

Our club has a policy about debate tournaments: The moment you get out of the car, your need to wear your game face. Any person you pass might be the judge in your next round, and you do not want to kick off a first impression with careless horseplay and silly jesting. You are always being watched and evaluated. Act accordingly.

Even if you never encounter your judge outside the round, the judge will be privy to everything you do once the round begins. If your partner is presenting, avoid distracting behavior or activity that makes you look vacant. Some debaters appear to be uninterested when they're not actually speaking. They drum their pens on the table, sway back and forth in their chairs or fix their gazes on a distant place. They chew their fingernails, fiddle with papers or doodle. Work to identify and eliminate these unintended distractions. Show interest in the speaker and respect for the judge's time by being actively engaged in the round.

When you're not speaking, pay attention to the other side's arguments. Listen to the questions your partner answers and consider how you will proceed after an admission. Be careful not to display reactions such as shaking your head, rolling your eyes, smiling victoriously, nodding or otherwise registering agreement or disagreement. Don't be a bobble head! And don't show exaggerated emotion. The judge is aware that there is a conflict and does not need you to highlight it. Maintain a dignified and respectful countenance and calmly take notes.

Make Eye Contact

"Look him in the eye" was probably the third directive I received as a young child after learning "please" and "thank you." If this is such a fundamental element of communication, why do so many debaters not make eye contact with their judges?

It's not enough to look up from your notes. Many debaters gaze at an indeterminate spot on the back wall or ceiling. Even in a large audience that is not enough, but it is especially deficient in debate rounds where a solitary judge represents the audience. You must look at your judge. In the eye. That is the only way to establish rapport and a connection with your judge. You are advising the judge, not merely speaking in the same room. To paraphrase federal judge Myron H. Bright, a fine speaker did not look the judge in the eye once, but delivered his entire argument looking down at his notes. Unfortunately for him, the wooden podium casts no vote.[15]

If you are speaking to a panel of judges, do not direct your entire advocacy at a single judge. Even if a particular judge shows more interest or is more engaged in the subject, every judge will cast a vote and therefore needs attention. Solicit each judge's attention in turn without emphasizing one over the others. Look from one judge to the next, making it clear that you are speaking to all of them.

Make Your Judge Like You

People tend to believe those who are like them. We are more amenable to persuasion when the advocate comes from the same background, has similar life experiences and looks like us.[16] Something we do in everyday social interactions is "mirror" or mimic those we are trying to persuade. When we like someone, we tend to mirror their movements and body language. This generally happens subconsciously (if you pay attention, you may see yourself doing it), but conscious efforts are just as effective. By acting like the person listening, we create a sense of empathy that opens the door to persuasion.

You can open this empathy door with your judge by mirroring hand gestures, leaning forward or away, or by copying head position. Psychology literature refers to this as the "persuasion mirror" or the "chameleon effect" and supports the notion that it can help connect with and persuade your judge.[17] Be subtle about it by inserting a delay of at least 2-4 seconds between the judge's movement and your mirroring. Be

---

[15] Bright, Myron H. (1975). *The Changing Nature of Federal Appeals.* 65 F.R.D. 496. p. 507.

[16] Van Swol, Lyn. (May, 2003). *The Effects of Nonverbal Mirroring With Persuasion and Agreement in a Group Discussion.* Paper presented at the annual meeting of the International Communication Association. See also *The Chameleon Effect: The Perception-Behavior Link and Social Interaction.* (1999). Journal of Personality and Social Psycholology. 76(6). pp. 893-910.

[17] *Ibid.*

careful not to turn the exercise into a charade, but do lean forward, put your elbow on the table or lean back to mirror your judge.

Even if you don't mange to mirror your judge perfectly, the act of keeping track of her movements means you will be plugged into her nonverbal feedback. You will be more in tune with her and be better able to gauge when she likes or detests an argument.

Tape Yourself

One of my students had the distracting habit of rocking back and forth when he presented. The movement relaxed him and his speech cadence followed his body like a metronome. Several coaches and I tried to tell him that the movement detracted from his delivery, but he was so comfortable rocking that he hardly noticed it.

So I put a digital video camera on a tripod and taped his presentation. When he watched it, he noticed his movement immediately. When he watched it fast-forwarded, the repetitive rocking was highlighted even more. He understood perfectly what was wrong once he saw it with his own eyes.

You are your own worst critic. When you listen to yourself speak or watch yourself present, you will know what is wrong. Record club drills or debate rounds and then watch yourself to self-diagnose delivery flaws and speaking faux pas.

Watch Other Cross-Examinations

Judging my first practice round as a senior in high school forever altered my perspective on debate. After some 350-odd rounds facing the judge, I finally had my moment on the other side of the podium. Being forced to adjudicate the round while giving feedback to the speakers gave me many new insights. I saw what worked and what did not—from the driver's seat.

Although you may not get the opportunity to judge a round until you graduate, you *can* watch debates. If you are eliminated in a tournament, make a point of watching outrounds. Wake up early (don't sleep in because you did not break, get to work improving yourself for the next tournament!) and go to all the outrounds you can. Put yourself in the position of the judge. Ask yourself how you would vote, what cross-examination tactics worked and which ones fell flat.

Outrounds typically proffer the best quality competition at a tournament. You should see some above-average cross-examination skills in these elimination rounds. Take note of how the successful debaters handle cross-examination. See if there are any routines you can adapt for your case or if there are any tactics that might work for you. One of the best ways to become good is to emulate the greats. Find out what's working and apply it yourself.

Cultivate a Reputation for Excellence

Skilled cross-examiners become known within the debate circuit. Competitors who are particularly adept at phrasing or navigating tough questions will generate conversation between rounds and tournaments. Debaters will recount their experiences against this excellent examiner, coaches will talk among themselves and to their competitors, and judges will rave to tournament directors. Expressions like, "That guy really knew his stuff," "I can't believe he made me say that" and, "How did she manage to squeak out of that?" all evidence your prowess.

Besides the ego- and confidence-boosting advantages of this kind of talk, having other debaters talk about you in a positive or admiring light may actually improve your cross-examination. You will find that admissions come more easily when you're known by your opponents as a tough examiner. Witnesses will be more tentative and less confident—if only slightly. The audience may create a buzz of anticipation before you get up to examine or the speaker may look nervous as you approach the podium.

The key is to make preparation a high priority. Practice using the drills in this book, develop lines of questioning to support your affirmative and negative arguments. Brainstorm responses to likely queries and memorize succinct answers. Ponder your strategy carefully and practice contingencies so you'll be able to move into your tactics seamlessly. Muscle through fatigue, discouragement and boredom. Even when you feel you have prepared as hard as you can, keep on working! You want to be as prepared as possible. You don't want to just win cross-examinations, you want to win them excellently.

Whatever the outcome of the round, the quality of your cross-examination will, in large part, determine the buzz you create. If you debate in the same judge pool on a regular basis, judges will recall your previous performances and view you as reasonable, reliable and trustworthy. If you have earned this reputation, your words will be given more consideration. You'll have an established credibility before you even begin the round. You want to be *known* as the speaker who puts *effort* into excellent cross-examinations.

Lincoln-Douglas Debaters during CX

CHAPTER **3**

Cross-Examination for the Witness

"In cross-examination, as in fishing, nothing is more ungainly than a fisherman pulled into the water by his catch." —Louis Nizer, trial attorney

When I work with students for the first time on cross-examination, I generally find that they are most unprepared to handle cross-examination as the witness. And, perhaps by extension of this lack of preparedness, they are also most afraid of answering questions. While an intuitive fear of cross-examination is understandable, especially if your image of the examiner is a shrewd, cutthroat prosecutor, the fact is that the witness has the most inherent authority of either party. The witness has just finished speaking, presenting evidence and otherwise introducing heady information. The witness has the podium, the credibility and the presence.

When the examiner steps up to question, the expectation is that the witness will cede the banner of authority. Effective witnesses defy this expectation. The witness must continue to appear to have all the answers and force the examiner to prove his credibility. The goal is not just to survive but to gain standing during the exchange.

Maintain Podium Control

You just finished a 6-8 minute speech. You have been presenting without competition for the judge's attention. The judge has probably been in a "zone" with you and is in tune with your delivery style. You have earned some credibility by introducing evidence, sound analysis or superior argumentation. The examiner is a newcomer to this persuasive relationship. He is interrupting your connection with the judge and, although courtesy requires that you extend some politeness, you would really rather be left alone.

Tradition says that you must give some podium space to your opponent. But there is no hard-and-fast rule about how *much* space you should give. Think of the podium (or lectern, music stand, etc.) as the demarcation of authority. The debaters sit on either side, but approach the podium in the center to speak to the judge. The nonverbal message you want to transmit to the judge is that the examiner is asking questions of the expert. *Two* experts are *not* engaging in verbal repartee. The examiner is asking questions of you, the expert. As the expert, you should continue to assert control over a majority share of the mantle of authority. Some debaters cede the entire podium to their opponent. This is certainly polite, but it is completely unnecessary and tells the judge that the examiner has the floor. Other debaters don't move at all, violating the expectation that the examiner deserves at least *some* consideration.

I advise that the examiner move over to give the examiner 25-40% of the podium, depending on the size difference between the competitors. If the witness is much bigger than the examiner, he will want to give more space. If the competitors are of equal size or if the witness is smaller than the examiner, hand over only a quarter of the podium. Maintain control over the podium to keep alive the authoritative momentum you have built in your speech.

Do Not Rock About

Once you have determined where you will stand and provided the requisite space for your opponent, do not move your feet or shift your weight back and forth. Movement creates abandoned space upon which the examiner may try to encroach. More likely, you will appear uncertain and shifty. Repetitive movement is distracting and creates an unfortunate contrast if your opponent is standing still. This is not a criticism of hand gestures. Maintain natural hand gestures while answering questions.

Come, Let Us Reason Together

Your want to convey the appearance of reasonability. The implicit message behind your arguments is that a reasonable person would agree with your stance. You want the judge to be invited into your ideas, not pushed away. You are asking the judge to come and reason with you.

The best way to send this message is by slowing down and lowering the pitch of your voice. High, shrill and fast tones do not invite the judge to reason. They do not make the judge a confident member of the discussion. You must speak, of course, with the voice God gave you, but pitch and speed can be trained. Don't exaggerate this until you speak like a late-night radio announcer or country singer Josh Turner, but realize that our natural tone tends to be elevated by excitement and passion. Back off that energy just enough so that the judge will feel welcomed by your answers.

Be Articulate

Cross-examination is not the time to drop consonants and slur your words. Speak with distinction. Practice enunciating each word clearly and separating them from the words before and after. The judge will not ask you to repeat yourself, so any words you slur or run together will not be caught. Speak clearly so that what you say will be heard and remembered.

Be Responsive

The one complaint judges most often report about witnesses is that their answers are not responsive. Judges are routinely frustrated by speakers who refuse to answer *point-blank* questions. Those who think they can avoid giving a straight answer by dodging are in for a surprise. As former Supreme Court Chief Justice Thurgood Marshall said, "nonresponsive and evasive answers merely invite the guillotine."[18]

---

[18] Marshall, Thurgood. (1968). *Counsel on Appeal.* (Arthur A. Carpenter ed.) p. 150.

It is *always* a mistake to evade obvious questions. The examiner will persist and you will end up spending even more time answering the tough query. Your evasiveness will draw the judge's attention to the weakness of your case. And when you finally cough out an answer, it will appear that the examiner worked hard for the admission. Your response will be much more costly than if you had confidently admitted the matter in the first place.

Respond in a way that does not invite the assumption that you have been defeated. Be calm and confident. State your position simply as if you have nothing to hide. Hopefully the judge will view your surefooted attitude as evidence that the admission was harmless. Think of the territory you want to evade like quicksand. You can struggle and fight, but your effort will only mire you. Confront every question squarely with your best answer. Evasion only plays into the hands of the skilled examiner.

Never Praise a Question

During my junior year in high school, I was examining my opponent in an elimination round. It went like this:

> *Q: So we've established that the Brookings evidence does not apply. Do you have any other solvency evidence indicating that your plan would produce the claimed advantages?*
>
> *A: That's a very good question. [witness fumbles with papers]*
>
> *Q: Thank you, but can you answer it?*

Never patronize your opponent with a trite "That's a good question" or "That's a tough one." The praise will not save you from the question and will highlight the query unnecessarily. The judge may not have thought it was a good question, but may now give your opponent more speaker points. *Answer* the question, don't *praise* it.

Prepare Zingers

An integral part of case development is to brainstorm and write *zingers* for your case. Zingers are short, paunchy phrases that support your case. They can be incorporated at any time to give your speeches extra zest or to transition between points. They are also very useful to you as a witness. When you write your case, think about a quick expression that you can use to help convey your main point. Is there a way to reintroduce your theme with a quick reference?

When my partner and I rawn a case to expand legal accountability for physicians' mistakes, we came up with these zingers:

1. Doctors' current attitude is, "Take two aspirin, go home and die."
2. The status quo is a wrist slap.
3. HMOs are medical gatekeepers.
4. Prescription, referral, treatment, the denials add up.

If the examiner marches a line of questioning toward your prepared, pithy phrase, feel confident letting it loose.

Don't Overstate Your Case

Your answers in cross-examination have to be oriented around the goal of improving your credibility. To paraphrase the Honorable Wiley Rutledge, Nothing, perhaps, so detracts from the force and persuasiveness of an argument as for the speaker to claim more than he is reasonably entitled to claim. Do not stretch evidence too far, making it appear to cover something to your benefit that it does not cover. Do not try to dodge or minimize unduly the facts which are against you. If one cannot win without doing this—and it is seldom he can by doing it—the position should not be argued.[19]

You have worked hard on your case—researching, brainstorming, practicing—and are probably convinced that you are right. Unfortunately, the judge lacks the benefit of this effort and is unlikely, at least initially, to be as gung ho as you. You harm your credibility and may be written off as a fanatic if you characterize your case as a slam dunk.

Even if you have undaunted confidence in your proposal, maintain a reasonable posture and tone while proceeding methodically through your answers. Do not say that your evidence supports more than it does.

---

[19] Rutledge, Wiley B. (1942). *The Appellate Brief.* 28 ABA J. 251. p. 254.

Recount facts from your speech accurately and honestly. Do not try to win arguments raised in cross-examination. An accurate recitation of the facts is more important than a skewed attempt at advocacy. If you do misrepresent facts, whether through carelessness or deliberate misstatement, your misrepresentation will likely be uncovered. And when you are exposed, you will suffer a grave loss of credibility.

Answer the "Hidden" Question

Many questions posed in cross-examinations are, for lack of a better term, *loaded*. They have a double meaning that may not be obvious during the query's introduction but becomes apparent later on. If you're arguing, for example, for a case granting lawful resident aliens certain government benefits, a likely question incorporates the assumption that your case would reward illegal aliens too. You should respond to the "hidden question" at the first opportunity.

> *Q: Does your plan grant aliens expanded rights?*
>
> *A: We aren't rewarding aliens for illegal activity, but we are trying to give them an equal economic footing.*

This is the politician's skill: the ability to respond to the latent or unstated meaning behind the question. To develop it, you need to think about what the examiner is going to do with the question. How will he apply the admission in the round? Why is he asking you this question? How does it relate to your case? If you have frequently debated your case, you may be familiar with common arguments and be able to better anticipate the direction of recurring questions. Perhaps you faced a similar hidden question in a practice round—do you have a good way of answering it now?

If you are pretty sure the examiner has a second meaning, start by quickly denying that meaning before answering the question. Make sure your response to its hidden insinuation comes before your answer to the stated question and that it is stated firmly, briefly and unequivocally. This will give you space to deal with it before the examiner cuts you off. Consider the following exchange where the examiner is negative against a case to ban assault weapons in the United States and is trying to set up a solvency argument:

Q: Do the authorities know the location of all the assault weapons in the United States?

A: No ... but law enforcement authorities—

Q: Thank you.

The witness is unable to answer the hidden question because the answer to the stated question came first. The champion witness answers like this:

Q: Do the authorities know the location of all the assault weapons in the United States?

A: Law enforcement keeps a database of registered guns and tracks their sale—

Q: Well, my question was if we know the location of all *the assault weapons.*

A: Not all of them, no.

Even as the examiner keeps close control of the cross-examination, the witness is able to mention the database of assault weapons. The judge will remember this exchange when the affirmative reads evidence about the database later on in the round. The admission may very well be rendered useless by the witness' shrewd answer to the hidden question.

State the Caveat Before the Admission

When examiners are not asking loaded questions, they may phrase their queries so that no absolute answer perfectly communicates your response. They may ask, "Are higher taxes undesirable?" or, "Is national security an important national priority?" These questions have obvious answers, but an unequivocal response is unlikely to explain the reservations you have on the topic. You may feel, for instance, that a tax hike is an undesirable but ultimately necessary fiscal policy move or that national security interests should be balanced with citizens' freedoms.

You need to introduce a caveat, or qualifying statement with your response. As with answering hidden questions, the key is to introduce the caveat *before* giving your substantive answer. You do not want the examiner to cut you off or move on after you say, "Yes, but—" Keep control of the cross-examination by saying, "A tax increase is necessary to adequately respond to the reasons for change described in our harms.

Taxes alone are not desirable, though." Or, "We need to balance national security against other interests in our policy-making like citizens freedoms and general welfare, but given that caveat it's definitely a priority."

Stating the caveat before the admission not only ensures that you will be allowed to introduce it without being cut off, it also lets you look smart. The issues broached in cross-examination are rarely as cut-and-dried as the examiner makes them seem. A detailed or multifaceted answer puts your nuanced understanding of the topic on display. You will appear to be the more intelligent person who better understands the difficulty and complexity of the arguments.

Confidently Answer "False Front" Questions

Many salespeople use a tactic of asking obvious questions that seem on their face to point to a conclusion. I remember one time in high school when my mother was purchasing a shirt for me, an enterprising (and very stout) salesclerk approached us with a matching tie combination that was, I must admit, rather dashing. My mother and the rep went back and forth about this and that, playing sales games that I am now just learning to understand, when the rep pulled me next to him, placed the shirt and tie next to me and said, "Doesn't he look great?"

Of course I looked great! I had taken a shower that morning and the back of my ears still felt clean from where I had scrubbed them. The salesperson's question had nothing to do with how *I* looked and everything to do with the shirt and tie. The fact that I look good was no great revelation and is, quite honestly, an entirely peripheral fact. The question's ingenuity was contained by its implicit conclusion: the shirt and tie would look great on your son.

More times then I care to recount, I have watched or judged a round with an examiner who was infatuated with such *false front* questions, that is, queries that sound significant at first blush but really are not. Still, if a witness is unprepared to handle these questions, they can be viciously effective. They tend to fluster and will spin evasive witnesses into a tizzy. Some debaters will even begin their routines with a passel of these questions to push their opponents on their heels before getting to the real meat. For instance, a case on granting illegal immigrants amnesty and citizenship might be met with the following false front questions:

> *Should those who do wrong be held responsible for their actions?*
>
> *Should lawbreakers be punished?*
>
> *In general, is it justified to ignore the law?*
>
> *Should laws be enforced?*

These questions appeal to an almost universally accepted value of rule of law and the natural respect for authority. The answers are therefore readily apparent and, at face value, really damaging. Of course those who do wrong should be held responsible, lawbreakers should be punished and laws enforced! What are rules if they can be trampled and laws if they can be ignored?

The witness's typical response is something like this ...

> *Q: Should those who do wrong be held responsible for their actions?*
>
> *A: Well, yes, but in our case—*
>
> *Examiner begins his next question.*

Waffling plays directly into the examiner's hands because it makes the witness appear unconfident and unresolved. An experienced examiner will never let an witness get more than a few words past the "but" before starting the next question. The judge has already heard the answer and hears just enough of a qualification to understand that the witness feels discomfited by it. The examiner is reasonably cutting off the witness and the audience is left with what appears to be agreement that "those who do wrong should be held responsible for their actions."

Take another look at the four questions above. Can debaters who agree on the answers to those questions disagree about whether amnesty should be given to illegal immigrants? The questions are so broad, so obvious, that they really do not pin the witness. They are harmless questions, designed to scare, not to garner admissions. Do not be afraid of them. Look the judge confidently in the eye and answer them unequivocally in a clear voice.

Sometimes false fronts are story questions that combine elements of values applied to unrelated fields. They *always* vastly underrepresent the complexity of the issues they handle. If you're faced with false front questions, treat them like your neighbor's Chihuahua that's always barking its head off, or the small child who screams bloody murder when she sees a worm. That is, regard them with a calm smile and a firm answer.

As long as there is common ground between your two teams, do not fear acknowledging the mutual turf in cross-examination. If your opponent tries to make a big deal of the things you both agree on, draw the judge's attention to all the things about which there is disagreement. The atheist and the Deist may agree on 90% of all epistemological topics, but the 10% they disagree on is very significant. The gravamen, or point of grievance in a debate is always the points of disagreement.

To finish the story I began to tell you about that matching shirt and tie, my mother ended up purchasing only the shirt, leaving the tie for another shopper. We saw through the salesman's false front questions and made our purchases based on reasoned analysis. When my mother and I talked before deciding for sure, we consciously addressed the rep's use of false front questions and concluded that one particular tie has only a minimal impact on how I look in general. Coincidentally, I saw the salesperson again a few weeks ago and we chatted amicably about the use of persuasion in clothes selling. He'd lost a few pounds, but one thing he said he would never leave behind is false front questions.

Confidently Answer Harmful Questions

You've been pinned into a corner. The examiner's skilled questions have eliminated all of your outs. Your efforts to avoid an admission have availed no credible escape. You're left with no choice but to give the examiner the admission he seeks. Even the best witnesses will be forced to provide an admission on occasion. Maybe your arguments are defective or contradictory. Perhaps you are outwitted by a smart strategy. The key to handling this eventuality is to answer *confidently*.

The worst way to admit an argument is to hem and haw, show defeated body language, tell the judge nonverbally that you are beaten and then speak in a humble whisper. This behavior brings undue attention to your admission. It is uncapping your rhetorical highlighter and telling the judge, "Remember this moment; I am beaten." Perhaps the judge would not have noticed the admission had you not drawn attention to it. More likely, the judge will think the admission is weightier than it is because of your defeated reaction and attitude.

The key to providing an admission is to do so in a confident, clear voice, as if nothing is the matter. You will feel your heart pounding like alpine thunder and your palms will sweat up a rain shower, but do not alter your cadence or delivery style. Do not phrase your affirmative response as a question or weaken your tone. If you maintain the appearance of confidence, the judge may never realize that the response was detrimental. If you smile calmly, the admission may be forgotten altogether.

Stick to the Oracle

In ancient Greece, the Oracle was a priest or priestess who made statements about future events. An Oracle's prophecies were believed to be infallible; no one dared question their veracity. In an argument, the ultimate rebuttal was "the Oracle said so," since no one dared cross the Oracle. Although not deemed as reliable as an Oracle, the equivalent in a debate round is the affirmative or negative case. When you answer questions, you want to always regard your case as the Oracle—and hold it in utmost regard.

Whenever your case contains an answer to a question, make reference to that fact in your response. Use phrases like, "As I said in my speech," or, "As my partner presented in the 1AC." Use them to introduce your answers when questions surface like, "How many people have been poisoned by asbestos in California?" or, "Has this plan ever been tried before?" Take pride in the credibility of your case and make an effort to show it off at every opportunity. Where possible, recite evidence. Say, "As the evidence from Henry Miller of the Hoover Institution said ..." or, "The Johns Hopkins study in my case demonstrated that ..."

Your credibility originated with your speech. Don't let it fizzle in cross-examination by feeling pressured to reinvent the wheel; the evidence and responses to the examiner's queries have probably already been presented. Refer back to them to adopt the credibility of the Oracle.

Adhere to the Defensible

Examiners sometimes like to take cross-examinations into sticky situations. They ask complicated hypothetical questions or focus queries on minute case details. Sometimes they ask questions designed to construct disadvantages that do not have any obvious case links. Other times they just go fishing. The key to maintaining control of the cross-examination is to insist on keeping questions on your defensible terrain. Watch for unreasonably tangential questions and call the examiner on them.

For example, in a case to abolish the death penalty:

> *Q: Each state has its own criminal sentencing guidelines, correct?*
>
> *A: You're missing the call of my argument. Our case is eliminating capital punishment for all states.*
>
> *Q: Sure, but each state uses different procedures to arrive at its criminal penalties, yes?*
>
> *A: I mean, that's still dodging the main point. The fact is that this is a federal issue, controlled by federal statute ...*

The witness may not know where the cross-examination is going. He does, however, understand that it won't matter what state policies are if capital punishment is abolished nationally. Since he is unfamiliar with the sentencing policy of all 50 states, he doesn't want to step into the minefield of, say, a Texas-specific disadvantage and suddenly find himself operating in the dark. The reasonable solution is to keep the cross-examination on defensible terrain. If the examiner keeps pushing, the witness can offer a convincing reply, such as:

> *Q: OK, but could you answer my question.*
>
> *A: I really can't speak to the state policies in general terms. My case is about the federal rule and the 8th Amendment's prohibition of cruel and unusual punishment.*

Every question asked of you as a witness must be viewed through the lens of the resolution and your case. As a witness, you are wearing a pair of livery blinders, pieces of black leather which direct a harnessed horse to look straight ahead. Peripheral questions may be answered, but only to the extent that they address something in your myopic visual range. Any question that has no application to your case is to be called out. Don't apologize for being unwilling to follow the examiner's rabbit trail. You came to the cross-examination expecting to answer questions about your case and the resolution. Even if the examiner has other ideas, stick to that defensible terrain.

Yield the Indefensible—Openly

Rarely will all the points in a debate round go in your favor. A reasonable advocate is comfortable acknowledging arguments that go against him. In fact, you should run out to meet the obvious indefensible points. To paraphrase the late constitutional and military law expert Frederick Bernays Wiener, Grasp your nettles firmly. No matter how unfavorable the facts are, they will hurt you more if the judge first learns them from your opponent. To gloss over a nasty fact is definitely harmful to the case. Draw the string of unpleasant facts by presenting them yourself.[20]

When my partner and I ran a case to allow medical malpractice lawsuits against health insurance companies, a routine disadvantage was that our plan would increase insurance premiums. The following cross-examination exchange was typical:

> *Q: Your case allows malpractice lawsuits against HMOs, right?*
>
> *A: Any managed care organization, yes.*
>
> *Q: Do malpractice lawsuits sometimes result in damage awards or financial settlements?*
>
> *A: Yes.*
>
> *Q: Will this increase insurance premiums?*
>
> *A: In Texas, our pilot project, insurance premiums went up by about 1.2%. In other cases, insureds saw an increase of 3-10 cents per month. So, yes, we anticipate a rise in insurance premiums.*

By agreeing that our case would result in an increase in premiums, we ran out to meet the argument. By referencing evidence in favor of that proposition, we told the judge we believed in the significance of our

---

[20] Wiener, Frederick Bernays. (1949). *Essentials of an Effective Appellate Brief.* 17 Geo. W. L. Rev. 143. p. 147.

harms so much that the disadvantage didn't scare us. Rather than deny an increase in premiums, an indefensible position, we yielded the tough ground to settle for a more reasonable posture. We "gave" the other side the argument, knowing we could still win our case. Hooray! thinks the judge, this is an honest debater.

So when the examiner asks questions with obvious answers, do not hesitate to give the sought answer. Common questions include, "Is genocide bad?" and, "Do you pay taxes?" By agreeing that genocide is bad, you are not necessarily endorsing the affirmative plan to intervene in Darfur. By acknowledging you pay taxes, you are not agreeing to the legitimacy of the income tax. If you try to waffle instead of ostentatiously yielding indefensible terrain, you will look unreasonable. Say, "Yes, genocide is a terrible atrocity," and, "Yes, I pay taxes." You will not have lost anything worth defending.

Beware the Admission Invitation

The questions start off easy and the answers are evident. You respond quickly and confidently, showing you know the topic. Each answer you provide leads to another question by the examiner. It is all so simple, so obvious. By the time you've noticed the trap, it's too late. You've given up an admission.

Skilled examiners will allow you to become comfortable with a line of questioning and then, once you've let down your guard, invite you to make an admission. Consider the following exchange where the examiner is running a case in favor of agriculture subsidies:

Q: Do you eat?

A: Yes.

Q: Do you like going hungry?

A: No.

Q: Do you think it's important to have a stable food supply?

A: Yes.

Q: Are domestic farmers integral to maintaining a stable food supply?

A: Yes, sure.

Q: Do we have a representative system of government?

A: Yes.

Q: Does the Constitution's preamble say we should promote the General Welfare?

A: Yes.

Q: Are you well if you are starving to death?

A: No.

Q: Are you well if you do not have a stable food supply?

A: No.

Q: Is it the government's duty to promote the General Welfare?

A: Yes.

Q: We can agree that it's the government's duty to maintain a stable food supply, right?

The examiner makes a lot of assumptions. He assumes that farmers rely on subsidies, that subsidies keep the food supply stable and that food-supply disruptions will result in starvation. He asks questions that are not relevant ("Do you eat?" "Do we have a representative government?") to make the witness more comfortable answering quickly. But a quick answer here could be a damning admission.

Whenever you hear "Of course," "We can agree" or "You concede," pause and think about how you got to this point. The examiner is inviting you to make an admission. Often the invitation will be the result of hasty responses, incomplete argumentation or fallacious assumptions. When the examiner asks if you agree or closes the line of question assumptively, assert your objections. In the example above, the skilled witness has lost nothing that cannot be regained with the following answer:

A: Look, you've made a bunch of assumptions in your questions. You've assumed that farmers rely on subsidies, that subsidies keep the food supply stable and that food-supply disruptions will result in starvation. We need to address these questions before deciding whether we agree or not.

Never Postpone a Response

Nothing kills the aura of credibility faster then an evasive answer like, “I'll have my partner bring that up,” or, “I'll look for details at the table.” As soon as a witness utters one of these infamous lines—or some variation on them—the judge, audience and other team assume that no answer is available and that the witness's team has no intention of ever addressing the issue again. Even if you are being honest, and you do actually have more details elsewhere, few will believe you. “I'll have my partner look into it” is a way of mitigating the damage of an “I don't know” answer. Any judge familiar with debate and even many who are not will instantly know what's going on.

The adage in cross-examination is that "later never comes." Invariably, a pledge to bring up a desired fact, figure or source will be forgotten as soon as the examiner says, "No further questions." The judge will conclude that you lack an effective response.

Examiners will try to get you to commit to using speech time to rectify errors made in cross-examination. A sign that an examiner has succeeded is when the witness uses rebuttal time to add to answers previously given in cross-examination. To avoid this, bring the debate to the examiner. If you do not have access to a fact, estimate it for the examiner ("Sure, but we have a recent study showing that something like one-third of jurors feel they would be better able to deliberate if they could take notes"). If evidence is out of reach at the table, describe it ("We have a card from a Federal Court of Appeals judge that contradicts that claim").

Retrieve Requested Evidence

When you bring the debate to the cross-examiner, she may ask questions that probe evidence not introduced in your speech. If you are answering questions about a document that is at the table, explain the nature of the document in detail without mentioning that it's not at the podium with you. If asked for details about your funding, for instance, describe the General Accounting Office report sitting a few feet away as accurately as your memory allows. If pressed for further details, presumptively move to pick up the document right then instead of pledging your partner's speech time for what is likely a fishing expedition by your opponent. For example, in a case on the U.S./Mexico border fence:

> *Q: Your plan mentioned a GAO report on funding; what was the date on that report?*
>
> *A: Uh, March 2008. It was referring to the previous fiscal year.*
>
> *Q: OK. Did that report deal with illegal immigrants living in all 50 states or just border states?*
>
> *A: Well, the introduction says it's about immigration in general, but I would have to look at the entire report to accurately answer your question. If you want, I can grab it for you.*
>
> *[Then immediately move toward your team's table to pick up the report.]*

Offering to retrieve the document during the cross-examination summons a few advantages. First, it costs the examiner time while earning you a few more credibility points. The examiner really cannot say no without looking hurried, concerned or allowing the argument to be written off as insignificant. Second, it moves attention away from the podium, relieving the tension of cross-examination and disrupting any flow the examiner may have established. Third, it puts the witness in control of the cross-examination by asking or implying a reasonable question that requires an answer. Most of the time the examiner is asking the questions, but he cannot avoid answering the subtle inquiry presented by a mobile witness.

Often when my students move to get evidence, examiners will get cold feet. They will back away from the question or move to another line entirely. This reaction shows how confident the witness, comfortably returning to the table, can be.

When You Don't Know, Say So

When the examiner digs to the end of your knowledge about a particular topic, the best answer is to admit that you do not have the answer. You are not expected to know everything and even with regard to a point you *should* know, acknowledged ignorance is better than proffered misinformation.

Instead of immediately offering the "partner's next speech" response, try the honesty approach. Believe it or not, one of the most credible things you can do as a speaker is reasonably admit you don't know something. If you have given all the details you can remember about a GAO report and are asked a narrow question about a study's methodology, feel free to give an honest "I'm not sure about that." This act of honesty will highlight all the things you do know as a speaker and make the facts you were able to recite more credible.

> *Q: OK. Did that report deal with illegal immigrants living in all 50 states or just border states?*
>
> *A: Hmmm ... I don't know.*

"I don't know" tells everyone that there are other things you *do* know, and that you're so comfortable in those things that you're unafraid to admit a lack of knowledge. At the end of the round, a judge will be much more likely to remember 30 seconds of fumbling than a two-second admission of ignorance.

After exhausting all reasonable wells of knowledge, the ability to admit you have reached the bottom is very credible. No one knows everything, so adding the touch of humanity that honesty brings can be very persuasive. Delaware lawyer and politician William Boyce put it best when he said, "If you don't know the answer, admit it; the penalty for not having an answer at your fingertips is less severe than the penalty for trying to fake it, getting caught, and giving the [examiner] an opportunity to bat you around like a cat playing with a ball of yarn."[21]

Have an Agenda

Have you ever tried to sell something to a door-to-door salesman? Pretty hard, isn't it? When people have a pressing matter on their mind or a specific goal dominating their psyche, it takes a lot to derail and reorient their thinking. A good examiner will have a clear purpose. Each inquiry will be crafted to paint the witness in a bad light or detract from the witness's credibility. You can diffuse an examiner's focused questioning by centering your answers on some neutral but largely irrelevant issue. It's called having an agenda.

---

[21] Boyce, William J. (2004). *Reflections on Going to the Show*. Report of the State Bar of Texas Appellate Section. p. 22-23.

You can use the door-to-door salesman principle to fluster and slow your opponent. If you have an agenda, you have someplace you want the cross-examination to go. This agenda necessarily conflicts with the examiner's since the three-minute time limit is too short to satisfy everyone's goals.

The agenda should be obscure, irrelevant and controversial. It must be obscure to ensure your opponent doesn't have any evidence to turn your answers against you. He should not be able to refute your agenda responses with a researched press. It should be irrelevant enough to have zero impact on the round, but at least tangentially close enough to the topic at hand to avoid being *non sequitur*. Finally, the agenda item should be controversial enough to justify any opinionated answer you choose to use it for. It should be a debatable concept that you can use both ways in cross-examination.

On the immigration topic, imagine if a witness decides to use the Immigration and Nationality Act as his agenda item. A cross-examination might go like this:

> *Q: Are immigration laws in America well enforced?*
>
> *A: It's interesting you should ask that. The Immigration and Nationality Act provides severe penalties for anyone caught violating federal immigration standards. The penalties are both civil and criminal and are much more extensive than those applied by the U.S. Immigration and Customs Enforcement agency, which is what most people look at when evaluating this topic.*

If you want to use the INA in support of the opposite position, you could say:

> *Q: You would agree that America's immigration laws are well enforced, wouldn't you?*
>
> *A: That question approaches the heart of a lot of controversy in our country. It's unfortunate that many Americans put a false confidence in their Immigration and Nationality Act which was supposed to extend severe penalties to ICE violators. In reality, many commentators believe that the law has left us more insecure as a half-million illegals flood into our nation each year.*

Whichever position you take, be sure to take it strongly. You do not want to be caught waffling on your own agenda item! Never say anything that is not true, but preface your comments with academic phrases that bear a universal veracity, such as, “Many feel,” or, “Some have argued.” If a topic is controversial, there will be those who "feel" and "argue" on both sides. You are not talking about anything relevant so you will not hurt your position with a few qualifiers, and the extra time serves to deplete your opponent's examination period.

Look for agenda items in federal and state legislation, executive orders, court rulings, international treaties and house resolutions. As you read about the topic, keep an eye peeled for obscure items that can be utilized as an agenda. When you find something, write it down.

If the examiner chooses to have a discussion on your agenda item and tries to disprove your position, you are in luck. The examiner has substituted your agenda for his; wouldn't you rather your opponent spend his time on a topic of your choosing then let him probe at will? Be as philosophical and helpful as possible. Research your agenda to the point that a few cross-examination questions will not reach the end of your understanding. And be sure to keep your agenda somewhat related to the question. Otherwise the strategy can backfire and lose the witness credibility. If the judge does not understand how the agenda is related to the examiner's question, you will look evasive and lose credibility. If you are naturally honest and open, the agenda will work very well for you.

Name-Drop

You do not want to be alone in cross-examination. So bring a buddy or three. Every source you cited in your speech, every expert you quoted is your friend. You adopt your sources' credibility when you invoke their names. In effect, you bring them out of the evidence and into the round with you. You do not need to reread the evidence, just refer back to it as if it is an old friend.

This tactic is especially effective for clarifying questions. When the examiner asks for the label of your second harm, say, "It's 'Unfunded Mandate.' I quoted Stanford law professor Larry Kramer on the dangers of forcing a state to enact a policy without allocating the money." When the examiner begins a line of questioning about your harm, he is pitting himself against you *and* a renowned constitutional law expert.

You can also respond to questions by speaking through your source, as your expert proxy.

> *Q: Aren't unfunded mandates common? I mean, the federal government does that fairly often, right?*
>
> *A: Professor Kramer would say that each instance is an unacceptable violation—*
>
> *Q: But it is fairly common, right?*
>
> *A: I'm not sure how often it's done. Look ... it's what The Economist called "the head ignoring the feet." Our harm is about the constitutionality not the scope.*

Feeling lonely in your cross-examination? Then invite your experts to join you. Incorporate sources from your speech by dropping names liberally.

Use Examples

Renee Berman was examined by five doctors after a cancerous tumor appeared on her liver. All five recommended immediate surgery. But a sixth doctor, who never examined Renee, denied her operation. This sixth physician was the head of a review committee for the health insurance company that refused to cover Renee's treatment. Renee's husband, Peter, blames this doctor and the managed care system for Renee's subsequent death. He told reform advocates Jamie Court and Francis Smith, "I blame my wife's death 20% on cancer and 80% on managed care."[22]

Renee's tragic passing touched my partner and I so much that we told her story in every round we debated in favor of reforming managed care policy. This example was a powerful presence during our speeches, but we made sure that it was incorporated into cross-examination, too. Whenever we answered questions about our harms, we made sure to incorporate Renee, even if we only mentioned her briefly. The following was typical:

> *Q: How expensive is discretionary treatment?*
>
> *A: It can get expensive; that's why you have insurance.*

---

[22] Court, Jamie and Smith, Francis. (1999). *Making a Killing: MCOs and the Threat to Your Health.* (Common Courage Press).

> *Q: So you're not concerned about saddling insurance companies with more cost?*
>
> *A: Insurance companies have a fiduciary obligation to pay for treatment. They can't abandon people like Renee Berman and not be held accountable.*

If your case follows a pilot project or was tried successfully by a state, mention that in cross-examination. If you had a persuasive example in your speech, reintroduce it. By referencing old examples, you keep them in your judge's mind and, with any luck, redirect the questions to your area of strength. You would rather talk about a pilot project or gripping anecdote from your case than probably any other area. If you can get your examiner to target this with his follow-up questions, you will quickly claim the higher ground.

Blame Confusion on the Examiner

Confusion is inevitable. Communication is hard enough without incorporating complicated policy and value topics while letting the speakers interrupt each other. Questions will be poorly phrased; answers will be misunderstood. The challenge for the witness is how to respond to confusion.

In theory, the examiner is in control of cross-examination. So when things go haywire, it is the examiner's fault. Never assume responsibility for the examiner's failure to keep control of the cross-examination, *even when you caused the breakdown*. If you don't understand a question, don't apologize for asking the examiner to rephrase. If the examiner misstates your response, interject without saying, "I'm sorry." If the examiner is struggling to find a question, wait patiently and stand silently. Confusion and breakdowns in communication are always the examiner's problem. Wait for him to sort it out.

Be Witty

Humor covers a host of sins. There's nothing like a witty comment to diffuse tension and show the confidence of the humorist. An appropriate joke will break the strain of even the most heated cross-examination. Actress and comedienne Phyllis Diller said, "A smile is a curve that sets everything straight." Look for opportunities to make light of the round or the examiner's questions. Incorporate a pun into your answer. Look for humor in the examiner's hypothetical question or in her follow-up queries. Some people are naturally funnier than others. If you have the gift of wit, incorporating humor will be much easier. Regardless, look for opportunities and capitalize.

An examiner in a nationals outround was trying to uncover the reason for a numerical discrepancy in the witness's evidence. Feeling that the problem was caused by different time frames, she asked:

> *Q: Your annual funding estimate was based on a fiscal year measure, right?*
>
> *A: You mean fiscal as opposed to the calendar year?*
>
> *Q: Yes.*
>
> *A: Correct, it is the fiscal year.*
>
> *Q: So when does the fiscal year start?*
>
> *A: October 1st.*
>
> *Q: And what year was that? [Referring to the publication date for the funding estimate evidence]*
>
> *A: Every year.*

In the ensuing laughter, nobody remembered the numerical discrepancy, not even the examiner.

To be witty, you need to feel relaxed enough to say whatever funny thought is on your mind. When wit rises to the tip of your tongue, let it fly—but don't eliminate all controls on your speech and automatically say something you might regret. The weapon of the Apostle James is dangerous and must not be left untamed. Don't avoid something *because* it's funny. But neither should you allow your humor to dominate your substance. As long as you're not too aggressive with your humor—a known hazard of wit—you should be fine.

Control the Pace

Skilled examiners develop a rhythm. Questions will arrive at a regular cadence. Each query will begin just as you finish your response to the last, giving you little time to catch your breath or reset mentally. By keeping the examination moving, the examiner is trying to force you off your game. The key is to control the pace.

The examiner cannot ask another question until you have answered the previous one. In essence, he will always be waiting for you. The cadence of your responses is the one thing in your power, so take control of it. Vary how much time you take to answer questions. Answer some questions quickly ("Sure") and take your time on others ("Hmmm ... yes"). By pausing before answering some questions and responding to others immediately, you assume a measure of control. Normal conversation endures regular tempo changes and pauses are commonplace. The rat-tat-tat of Gatling gun cross-examination would be unnatural at the dinner table. No one will fault you for taking a breath in a debate round.

If you're still feeling pressured after alternating your response times, try considering each question as its own query, independent of previous responses. Measure your response in your mind and consider its phrasing. Does the examiner need to clarify the question? Can you object to the query? Show the judge your thinking by squinting your eyes and pursing your lips or taking a medium breath. And don't wait to do this until you've hit a question you're unsure about. If you take time for questions you can answer confidently, you will be able to reasonably take a second for the harder ones.

Do Not Repeat Questions

You control the pace through pausing and tempo changes—not by repeating the examiner's questions. Repeating questions is commonly cited as a verbal signal that you're about to tell a lie.[23] It makes you look unconfident *and* highlights the examiner's question, thereby reducing your ability to credibly waffle or use an agenda. It shows the judge you are unprepared for the question. And it can be downright irritating. If you do not understand the question, identify the area of ambiguity and ask the examiner to rephrase. If you did not hear a question, ask the examiner to repeat it. But don't repeat it yourself.

---

[23] Adelson, Rachel. (August, 2004). "Detecting Deception." *APA Monitor*. Vol. 35, No. 7. p. 70.

Never Back Away From Your Sources

My partner and I were in the final round, facing off against one of the state's best teams who ran a case to amend the Earned Income Tax Credit in Puerto Rico. In my constructive, I depended heavily on one source for the bulk of my solvency and disadvantage arguments. I didn't notice that that same source had figured prominently in the affirmative's case, setting up an epic cross-examination clash.

When you present a source in a debate round, it becomes your Bible. You will rally around that source, defend its credentials and generally build it up. You will protect that source the way you would a closest loved one. It is your main advocate and you should never back away. With this principle firmly in mind, I invited cross-examination. It went something like this:

> *Q: So, Cody, what source did you quote under your solvency arguments?*
>
> *A: I quoted Mary McCullough, an expert in tax law and policy.*
>
> *Q: So you think Mary McCullough is qualified to talk about protectorate policy?*
>
> *A: Absolutely, yes. She has her PhD in public policy and an LLM in tax law. She has published articles about Puerto Rico for the last couple decades.*
>
> *Q: Cody, can you tell me what Mary McCullough's conclusion was—what was the conclusion on her study?*
>
> *A: I'm not sure.*
>
> *Q: If I were to represent to you that she concludes by advocating the change in our plan, would that impact your solvency?*
>
> *A: Even if Mary McCullough draws a different conclusion, she is raising some serious objections that need to be addressed. We are debating here to persuade the judges and Mary McCullough raises some valid concerns in her article regardless of her conclusion.*

I might have balked and retreated from the source. I might have referenced the "multitude of other sources that support this position" or promised that my partner would bring up more evidence, implying that the sources already presented were somehow deficient. All of these strategies required retreating from the evidence. There is little doubt that the McCullough evidence was flawed. It was probably a mistake to present it in the debate round—we should have known her conclusions. But backing away from the source in cross-examination would only have compounded the problem.

All the judges, by the way, ended up voting negative on the solvency arguments that were heavily reliant on the McCullough evidence. Had I backed away from the evidence in cross-examination, things would probably have turned out very differently.

Your Response Is Fact

Examiners ask questions like:

– *Do you think oil price fluctuations are too volatile?*

– *In your opinion, should net benefits be the criterion for today's round?*

– *Do you value sanctity of life over the quality life?*

When you answer, avoid the first person singular (I, me) and any sentence construction that implies the answer is held only by you. Do not say, "I think," "The affirmative's position is" or "In our view." These expressions make your response seem like it is nothing more than your *opinion*. Also, depending on inflection and circumstance, use of the first person can make you sound arrogant and pompous. The first person certainly does not make you sound sure of yourself. So state your response as fact, not opinion.

Avoid Categorical Answers

Is it wrong to kill? At what temperature does water boil? Should citizens pay taxes levied by their government? For fun, I posed these and other categorical questions to a professor of philosophy at my undergraduate university. I felt like Billy the Kid shooting my six-gun at the heels of the tenderfoot to "make him dance." But my professor agilely dodged every slug. Killing is wrong when it lacks "moral justification." The boiling point of water depends on altitude and air pressure. A citizens' obligation is much too complicated to give a simple yes or no to the tax question.

If our teachers can avoid giving categorical answers, why can't witnesses, especially witnesses who should be acting like teachers? Categorical questions appear must prominently in values debate, although they are introduced in policy rounds. The key to handling them is to first invite the judge into the complexity of the question. Use a phrase like, "That's a question that's been debated throughout the ages," or, "You have just now distilled five centuries of political thought into one yes or no question." Once you have explained that the question is multifaceted or does not admit one easy answer, you can explain your position more carefully.

> *Q: Is it wrong to kill?*
>
> *A: You know, that's a question that's been debated throughout the ages. Let me see if I can give a simple answer: By default, killing is a moral wrong, but there are circumstances that justify deadly force, like self-defense. You have to balance the victim's right to life against his actions. Sometimes that calculus justifies killing.*

Clarify the Question

Former chief justice William Rehnquist said, "If you are going to be able to intelligently answer a question, you must first listen to the question. ... Just like many private conversations, people seem to hear only part of the question, and respond to the part of it they heard even though the answer they give may not be an adequate response to the entire question."[24] In cross-examination, much time is wasted and credibility lost when witnesses launch into an answer to a question that is substantially different from the one the examiner actually posed. Make sure you have a solid understanding of the question, then, before introducing your answer.

If you think you understand the question, but aren't sure, begin by saying, "If I understand your question correctly, you are asking whether ..." Do not restate the question to make it easier, but do use simpler phrasing if it is available. Intelligent conversation requires that you listen carefully. If you are not sure about the examiner's intent, *clarify*.

---

[24] Rehnquist, William H. (1986). *Oral Advocacy.* 27 S. Tex. L. Rev. 289. p. 302.

Let Your Passion Show Through

If you watch a debate round carefully, you will notice that most witnesses adopt a different style of delivery than they assumed during their speech. Oratorical speakers become less excited; analytical debaters more conversational. Fast speakers slow down. Cross-examination has a moderating effect on delivery.

While there is nothing inherently wrong with changing the way you communicate while answering questions, you need to make sure that your passion for the topic and excitement for the case continue to show through. Do not stop being persuasive simply because someone else is at the podium with you. Show your enthusiasm for the case and topic with your word choices and animated expression. Don't forget why you fell in love with your case. Recall what first drew you to the plan action or the need you recognized and wrote into the harms. Make sure you are communicating that emotion before, during and after cross-examination.

Stop Talking When You Are Cut Off

Cross-examiners like to cut off witnesses. Some will say "thank you" or begin their next question as soon as they get the answer they want, whether or not the witness is done responding. To many witnesses this is frustrating. Some will look annoyed, roll their eyes or shift their weight. Others will plow right through the examiner in an attempt to complete their answer. Great witnesses stop talking and stand still as soon as they are interrupted.

A rule of thumb for public speaking is that the silent person is the one with the power. In the competitive exchange of cross-examination, it often looks like the speakers are fighting each other for air time, as if the person who fills the air the most wins. Lost in this avalanche of words is a true sense of authority. Only a confident speaker can stand in front of a group of people and pause. Even though it is a natural part of communication, dead air makes us uncomfortable. At a subconscious level, we expect our opponent or an audience member to step up and take our place. Confidence, authority and power are demonstrated when you are willing to stay silent.

Stop talking immediately when the examiner says anything during your response. Stopping quickly draws attention to the fact that you've been interrupted. You're not annoyed by the interruption, just silenced. Like a teacher whose pupil has interjected something, you stop to listen but keep the mantle of authority. The first time you halt may be awkward. The examiner might not have another question prepared or might not be expecting you to halt so readily. Over time, examiners will generally give you more leeway knowing that you are so willing to stop. Examiners who abuse your politeness will look rude and sharkish. Judges will be impressed by your confidence and turned off by the examiner's intensity.

Answer the Last Question Briefly

When the timer announces the expiration of cross-examination, finish answering the last question posed. But be as succinct as possible and do not abuse the time call by pontificating. Some examiners will keep asking questions after time has expired. The judge will mark the examiner down for this behavior. It's not your job to point to the timer and ask the judge to stop the cross-examination. Remember that you want to appear comfortable and confident. Demanding recess is not the way to convey that perspective. Keep on answering questions until the judge tells you to stop or the examiner ceases.

Lawyers' Objections

"Anger blows out the lamp of the mind. In the examination of a great and important question, every one should be serene, slow-pulsed, and calm." —Charles J. Ingersoll, lawyer and politician

When a witness answers questions in a courtroom setting, a licensed attorney is present. The lawyer listens to the questions, weighing the demands of the queries against the rules regulating cross-examination and the witness's rights. The lawyer will, on occasion, object, state some rule or right that the question abrogates and ask that the query be withdrawn or amended. Objections—though one of the witness's chief defenses in the legal world—are absent in academic forensics. You don't have a lawyer, so you must defend your own rights.

If a question is objectionable, state the objection and ask your opponent to rephrase it. Say, "Your question is compound, can you rephrase it?" or, "Your question is irrelevant in the context of the topic, can you rephrase it so that it relates to my case?" If the examiner's rephrased question is still objectionable, be ready to provide more details. Say, "You asked me this same question a minute ago. My answer that [insert earlier response] has not changed," or, "Your question is vague because you did not specify what you mean by 'significant increase.' You would need to quantify that for your question to be answerable."

If these objections appear cold and harsh, remember that they are designed for the courtroom. You do not need to be snooty or haughty when you introduce them—a bad attitude will repel your judge—but you do need to be firm. Like a skilled lawyer, you are protecting your rights as a speaker, not just objecting for the thrill of it. Give the examiner an out by asking him to rephrase his question, but do not answer flawed questions and certainly do not apologize for them.

Ambiguous, Unintelligible, Confusing, Misleading, Vague

> *"Your question is ambiguous, can you rephrase it please?"*
>
> *"As it is currently phrased, your question is misleading. It confuses two key terms in our case."*
>
> *"I don't understand your question, can you ask it another way?"*

Any of these is a proper objection to a question not posed in a clear and precise manner. Before you can answer, you must know with certainty what's being asked. If you are unsure about what the examiner means by a particular term, expression or implication, ask.

Argumentative

> *"That's a statement, can you state it as a question?"*
>
> *"That sounds like an argument. Do you have a question for me?"*

In an argumentative question, the examiner states a conclusion and then asks the witness to argue with it. The examiner may be trying to get the witness to change an earlier response or might simply be engaging in argument during the cross-examination. It a courtroom, this would be called arguing with or badgering the witness and would be disallowed. You are under no compunction to answer argumentative questions. Your opponent can be forceful and pressing but if the questions devolve into arguments, object.

Asked and Answered

"You asked me this a minute ago, my answer is the same."

"This question is no different than the one your partner put to mine. Our answer is the same."

Examiners will often try to emphasize a point by repeating the question that elicited a crucial answer. If the examiner asks you to rephrase your previous testimony, you may do so. But introducing the "asked and answered" objection shows that you have been paying attention to the cross-examination.

Assumes Facts Not in Evidence

"Your question assumes that our plan will increase the risk of a terrorist attack. There is no evidence for this assumption."

"You are assuming a fact not in evidence by indicating that your plan will actually change people's behavior."

This objection is used when the introductory part of a question assumes the truth of a fact that is in dispute.

Beyond the Scope

"This question takes us beyond the scope of the round."

"This question is not related to the arguments in the round or my case in general. Can you relate it back for me?

If the resolution presents the limits for the round, you can reasonably object to any question that takes you beyond those limits.

Compound Question

> *"You seem to be asking a couple questions at once. Can you ask them one at a time?"*
>
> *"Are you asking me [Question 1] or [Question 2]?"*

A compound question asks two or more separate questions within the framework of a single query. A simple test for a compound question is if the witness answers "no," would the judge be confused about which part of the question is being answered?

False Dichotomy

> *"Your question poses a false dichotomy. It gives two unacceptable options. Can you rephrase?"*
>
> *"You gave me two options, the truth is option three."*
>
> *"Neither."*

A false dichotomy presents a choice between two or more unacceptable options. A classic false dichotomy is the question, "Have you stopped beating your wife?" "Yes" admits a history of beating. "No" suggests that the behavior continues. You may either object to false dichotomies or say "neither" and wait for the examiner to ask a question that gives you the chance to clarify.

CHAPTER 4

Triage, Trees and Prioritization*

"Luck is when preparation meets opportunity." —Seneca, Roman philosopher and politician

In the chapters that follow, we delve into the examiner's *tactics*. We explore effective interrogation techniques that will aid in the design and presentation of questions and lines of questions in a particular cross-examination session. You will find that the tactics discussed are too numerous to all be applied in a single cross-examination. So expansive are these keys that you will have to pick and choose what to use in a given round.

To help you do that, I'll start with the *strategy* of cross-examination. Strategy means a coordinating paradigm or model that governs the selection and organization of tactical rules. Below we will tackle the strategic problems inherent in a time-limited activity by developing a model for you to choose and write your questions.

Triage of Inquiry

The terror of war and its resulting devastation first motivated the use of medical triage. Although experts differ on who first developed the idea and the practice was probably undertaken under other appellations in pre-20th-century conflicts, the concept was first formalized in World War

* Chapter adapted from a paper by Alan Cirlin, presented at the Annual Meeting of the Speech Communication Association (74th, New Orleans, LA, November 3-6, 1988), titled *On the Strategy of Cross Examination.*

I by French doctors treating the battlefield wounded at aid stations located behind the front.[25] After a battle, as casualties were carted into hospital tents, nurses had to make quick decisions about how to allocate scarce medical resources. There simply were not enough doctors to treat everyone. So the nurses divided up the wounded into three categories:

1) Those who were likely to live regardless of what care they received;

2) Those who were likely to die regardless of what care they received; and

3) Those for whom immediate care might make a positive difference in outcome.[26]

Like medical care in war, in cross-examination, time and your credibility are scarce resources. You cannot keep asking questions for 10 minutes. And your judge will stop taking you seriously if you target irrelevant topics or badger the witness abusively. In the analogy, each argument is a wounded soldier approaching the cross-examination hospital tent. As the examiner, you are the triage nurse charged with evaluating the vitality of each argument.

At the triage tent, the wounded that fall in the first and second categories are put aside. Soldiers in the first category—those likely to live regardless of care—are not critical. They can be shipped home and treated at a hospital with more resources. Arguments that you are likely to win regardless of how things go in cross-examination are generally not worth the effort of address. Wounded in the second category—those likely to die regardless of care—are not worth treating since resources bestowed upon them are wasted. In the crude world of battlefield triage, they are left to die. Arguments that you are very unlikely to win no matter what you do are, likewise, usually a waste of time in cross-examination. There is no reason to try to revive them.

Soldiers in the third category—those for whom immediate care could make all the difference—are important both for the hospital tent and for your cross-examination. It his here that you should concentrate your

---

[25] Iserson, K. and Moskop, J. *Triage in Medicine, Part I: Concept, History, and Types*. Annals of Emergency Medicine. Volume 49, Issue 3, pp. 275-281.

[26] Chipman, M, Hackley, B.E., and Spencer, T.S. (1980). *Triage of Mass Casualties: Concepts for Coping With Mixed Battlefield Injuries*. Military Medicine. 145(2). pp. 99-100.

efforts. The key is to maximize your effectiveness. Your questions will have more utility if they follow the rules of triage.

Arguments

The notion of prioritizing questions through triage is only half the model. Winning debaters need to also prioritize their chosen arguments. Without a weighing mechanism for arguments, effective triage of inquiry is impossible.

The problem with arguments is that they are actually much more complicated than a wounded soldier. Distinguish in your mind, for a moment, an argument about illegal immigration. In a debate round, it might be said something like this:

> "Illegal immigrants are crossing our border more now than ever before. Today, one sixth of the Mexican work force now works in the United States. That is 10% of Mexico's population. The influx of immigrants has taken American jobs and increased our national unemployment rate. If immigration laws were effectively enforced, the number of low-skilled jobs available to American citizens would increase and the unemployment rate would fall."

This is a fairly simple argument claiming that because illegal immigrants take low-skilled American jobs, causing a rise in unemployment, enforcing immigration rules would reduce unemployment. We can state this formally using a simplified Toulmin model as follows:

Claim: "Effective enforcement of immigration laws would reduce unemployment."

Grounds (evidence): "Today, one sixth of the Mexican work force now works in the United States. That is 10% of Mexico's population." And (implicitly), "Effective enforcement of immigration laws would force illegal immigrants to leave the country."

Warrant (assumed in this case): "American workers are ready and able to accept the low-skilled jobs abandoned by deported illegal immigrants."

At this point the argument is not very complicated. But as soon as cross-examination begins, it can quickly become unmanageable. Since most cross-examination answers present a choice among many alternatives as directed by the questioner, the possible courses of the cross-examination session usually expands from answer to answer. In other words, the argument is at first limited to the two explicitly stated elements distinguished above. But once cross-examination begins, the implicit elements are automatically in play. The examiner can also pose a hypothetical or develop an analogous line of reasoning on a tangentially related topic. Every response the witness proffers generates more question opportunities which, in turn, admit more possible responses.

This gets confusing quickly. There has to be some way to simplify it into a useful model so we can triage our arguments and design effective cross-examinations.

The late philosophical genius Stephen Toulmin was upset with the complexity of formal logic. He claimed it was too abstract and did not accurately represent the way human beings actually argue. To make up for these perceived deficiencies, he developed the Toulmin model. Today, this model is important for every debater to understand the structure and composition of arguments:

A **CLAIM** is the point a proponent is trying to make. It is the proposition that you want others to accept. If someone where to interrupt you in the middle of your argument and ask, "So, what's your point?" you would reply with your claim. Examples of claims include:

> *"We should never take another person's life."*
>
> *"We should try to reduce the national debt."*
>
> *"Because of gravity, objects with mass are attracted to one another."*

Toulmin divides these claims into three basic types. *Judgment, or value claims* involve opinions, attitudes and the subjective evaluation of things. Saying that "human life is sacred" is a value claim. *Policy claims* advocate particular courses of action. The statement about national debt is a policy claim. *Fact claims* are about empirically verifiable phenomena. We can test gravity, therefore it is a claim related to fact.

The second element of the Toulmin model is **GROUNDS**. Grounds refers to the proof or evidence proffered in support of a claim. If someone asks,

"How do you know that?" or, "Why?" or, "What is your evidence?" you would answer with your grounds. This element of an argument can consist of statistics, quotations from experts, findings from studies, evidence from observation and various forms of reasoning. Examples of grounds include:

> *"There is a transcendent moral dignity inherent in every life. This dignity differentiates human life from all other life forms."*
>
> *"According to Richard Rahn, a senior fellow at the Cato Institute and chairman of the Institute for Global Economic Growth, maintaining the national debt at its current elevated level is 'foolish and destructive.'"*[27]
>
> *"I dropped a ball 10 times yesterday and it went down every time it left my hand. It never went up."*

Toulmin's biggest contribution to the field of forensics logic came in the form of his third element, the **WARRANT**. A warrant is the "inferential leap" that connects the claim to the grounds. Warrants are typically not explicitly stated, although they can be. The alert opponent will listen for the warrant and may explicitly identify the underlying reasoning of the argument when providing refutation. Examples of warrants include:

> *"Because human life is sacred, it should never be taken."*
>
> *"We should take the expert Rahn at his word when he says that increasing the national debt is unwise."*
>
> *"Given my previous observations on the physical performance of the ball I dropped yesterday and the uniform behavior exhibited by the ball as it left my hand, I expect all objects with mass to perform similarly."*

Toulmin categorized arguments by the kind of warrant they employ. To help design these categories, he introduced us to some terms first employed by Greek philosopher Aristotle to evaluate arguments:

Warrants based on Ethos Appeal. Ethos means convincing by the character of the author. It's inexorably linked to your credibility. People tend to believe those whom they respect. By associating yourself with someone the judge believes is worth listening to, you can gain some of that worthy

---

[27] Rahn, Richard. (September 22, 2009). *The Growing Debt Bomb.* Washington Times.

person's authority. The argument about the national debt, above, employs an Ethos warrant.

Warrants based on Logos Appeal. Logos means persuading by the use of logic, or reasoning. This was Aristotle's favorite, and it is the hardest to master. Warrants based on logic generally use a "proof" (inductive or deductive) to link the grounds to the claim. The argument about gravity employs a Logos warrant.

Warrants based on Pathos Appeal. Pathos means persuading by appealing to the listener's emotions or by appealing to such shared values as free speech, fairness, dignity, etc. Language choice and delivery style are among the things that affect a judge's emotional response and can effectively be used to enhance this warrant. The argument about the sanctity of life employs a Pathos warrant.

This is a greatly simplified explanation of the Toulmin model. Studying the model in depth will improve your ability to analyze and respond to argumentation. I highly recommend that you read Toulmin's 1969 book, *The Uses of Argument,* published by Cambridge University Press. Also helpful is Austin J. Freeley's 2008 tome, *Argumentation and Debate,* from Wadsworth Publishing.

Cross-Examination Trees

The *Handbook of Industrial Engineering* provides us with a very useful tool by offering up the delightfully simple idea of a "decision tree."[28] If you write down all the possible paths the cross-examination might take, the resulting graph would resemble a continually branching diagram or tree. "Instead of compressing all the information regarding a complicated [problem] into a table," say the handbooks authors, J.R. Buck and J.M.A. Tanchoco, "one draws a schematic representation of the problem that displays the information in a more easily understood fashion.[29]

---

[28] Buck, J.R. and Tanchoco, J.M.A. (1982). "Economic Risk Analysis," in *Handbook of Industrial Engineering*. (Wiley & Sons: New York, NY). p. 53.

[29] *Id.*

The decision tree allows the examiner to anticipate the witness's answer and develop follow-up queries. In the low-stress privacy of the witness's home, away from the waving fingers of the timer and beady glare of an impatient judge, examiners can use virtually unlimited prep time to prepare their trees.

To develop a cross-examination tree, start by writing down the goal of your line of questioning. Your goal is the admission or response you want to illicit from the witness. Some admissions are fairly obvious from listening to the affirmative case and you only need to ask one question to highlight a fact for your audience ("Did you specify a source of funding in your plan?" "Did you address my second contention?"). Other questions require a series of setup or preliminary questions that serve to create the foundation for your main query.

Your setup questions will generally fall into three categories. Leading questions suggest or contain the answer you are looking for ("The FDA regulates the approval of new drugs in the United States, right?" "Is it true that federal policy makers should be concerned about protecting the environment?"). In most U.S. courtrooms, leading questions are allowed during the examination of hostile or opposing witnesses. They are also allowed in debate competitions. You should expect your opponent to be as evasive as a hostile witness, and that means you should write questions that include guidance regarding your desired response.

The second category of setup questions are trap questions. These are questions that "force" your opponent to answer one way to avoid looking bad or contradicting himself. For example, you could ask, "Is human life important?" You expect the witness to answer "yes," but you should be ready with a quick follow-up ("So you wouldn't mind if we all lost our right to life?") if you're given anything other than a satisfactory answer.

Finally, you can ask questions seeking factual responses to specifically worded questions. Examples include: "What is the population of the United States?" and, "What is the penalty for violating the EPA regulations discussed in your case?" These questions do not allow much room to waffle, since the examiner will have to stick with a simple factual recitation or admit lack of knowledge.

There are two caveats regarding questions seeking factual responses. First, do not ask factual questions the witness would not be reasonably prepared to answer. Questions about the details of the team's case are fine—people are expected to know their own case—but queries about your own case or specific knowledge outside the realm of the topic being discussed invite either smart responses or reasonable "I don't knows." I heard about a cross-examination that had a senior examining a freshman. The senior tried to intimidate the witness by asking, "How many dimples are there on a golf ball?" The freshman was unfazed as she answered, "Wilson or Spalding?" An "I don't know" would have sufficed as well, although it would have been less memorable.

The second caveat is to beware the evasive "I don't know." Evasive witnesses will sometimes plead ignorance to avoid explicitly stating something damning to their case. If you suspect that an "I don't know" is being used falsely or if you really need to have some kind of response to continue that line of questioning, consider asking for an estimate ("Can you estimate for me, then, the number of farmers in the United States?") or offering the correct answer as assistance ("If I represent to you that there are about 1 million farmers in the United States, would you agree?").

With all setup questions, you should have a general idea of how the witness is going to respond. An old lawyer adage is to "never ask a question you don't know the answer to." To be in control, you need to have a general idea of where things are going. And when you *are* unsure how the witness will respond, you should have contingent follow-up questions prepared.

A cross-examination tree designed to illicit an admission to support the unemployment/illegal immigration argument above might look something like this:

> *Q: What kind of work do illegal immigrants typically perform?*
>
> *A: Generally manual labor and low-skilled jobs. Immigrants who have worker visas are more likely to perform skilled work.*
>
> *Q: Are there unemployed workers in the United States?*
>
> *A: Yes.*
>
> *Q: What percent of the Mexican workforce is in the United States?*
>
> *A: I'm not sure ... about a tenth.*
>
> *Q: Would you say it's a significant percentage?*

A: A significant minority, sure.

Q: What is the unemployment rate in the United States?

A: It depends on the part of the country—

Q: Nationally. What is the national unemployment rate?

A: About 10% or so.

The examiner cannot ask, "Are American workers willing to perform the tasks currently undertaken by illegal immigrants?" because this is the lynchpin of the argument. The witness will obviously say "no," and the line of questioning will be dead. Instead, you have to tiptoe around the point by asking everything but the ultimate question. You'll have time in your speech later to complete the picture and win the argument.

Predicting the Witness's Move

The most difficult aspect of formulating a decision tree is the difficulty inherent in accurately predicting the course of a cross-examination. Accuracy drops off quickly the deeper into the tree the cross-examination goes. Some coaches suggest this is why inexperienced debaters can be completely lost in cross-examination. It's not that they have nothing to say, it's that they are, in debate-minded author Alan Cirlin's words, "completely adrift in a vast sea of possible things to say. Questioners can not decide among the multitude of possible techniques they have been taught and respondents cannot cope [with] the countless variations inherent in their choice of answer."[30]

The problem is too substantial to be resolved by contingency-plan coaching and rote memorization. Debaters who learn what to do next while ignoring *why* it is the appropriate move are especially prone to fall into this trap. But examiners can limit the potential damage. ...

No Open-Ended Questions

The best way to predict where your witness will go next is to limit her exit options. If you can construct a sturdy cage with your questions, you

---

30 Cirlin, *supra*, at p. 6.

will have no problem freeing a bird in its confines. What that means is this: The key to developing a usable and effective cross-examination tree is to fashion questions that do not admit a multiplicity of possible answers.

You do not want to ask open-ended questions that give the witness many reasonable responses. Open-ended questions make it nearly impossible to accurately plan follow-up queries or to adhere to any kind of preparation. You simply do not know where the witness will take the response and, by extension, the cross-examination. Consider the following question, designed to set up a politics disadvantage:

> *Q: Why did Congress choose not to pass the immigration reform bill?*
>
> *A: Oil prices rose substantially the month before the vote and Majority Leader Harry Reid tabled the debate on S.B. 213. Had oil prices not gone up so much, we might not have our inherency today.*

The examiner is unable to use this response to establish political backlash against a bill mandating the use of an Internet database to verify employees' legal status. If anything, the witness now has a response to at least one of the links to the disadvantage (the Senate's inaction does not mean opposition) in front of the judge.

An admission could have been more effectively garnered as follows:

> *Q: Has the Senate passed S.B. 213?*
>
> *A: No.*
>
> *Q: Has the Senate voted on any E-Verify bill this session?*
>
> *A: I'm not sure.*
>
> *Q: So you're not aware of any E-Verify bill that the Senate has voted on this session?*
>
> *A: No.*

What Should I Ask First?

Earlier we discussed the role of particular cross-examination questions. Let's review them again:

1) To enhance one's own or to detract from one's opponent's Ethos;

2) To further one's own or to detract from one's opponent's emotional position;

3) To defend one's own or to attack one's opponent's logical reasoning and evidence; and

4) To further one's own or attack one's opponent's case perspective.

As you listen to your opponent's case, ask yourself whether you understand the thesis being advocated. Do you understand the basic mechanisms of the affirmative's case? Do you follow the basic mechanisms of the negative objections? If you do not understand the other debater's thesis, then questions of clarification deserve the highest priority. Examples of these questions include:

> *Q: In one sentence, can you describe your plan action?*
>
> *Q: Are you arguing that increasing taxes on cigarettes would reduce cigarette consumption?*
>
> *Q: Essentially your case thesis is that keeping illegal immigrants out of the United States would benefit American workers, do I have that right?*

Your second priority is to understand the main points of your opponent's case. As the negative, evaluate whether you have the affirmative's case superstructure. As the affirmative, see if you understand the major points of the negative's argumentation. You can ask for a copy of the affirmative case, but if any major points are still vague, cross-examination is the time to ask for clarification. If everything is clear and you are sure you know what your opponent is arguing, you can begin asking the tough questions.

Debaters often wonder where they should ask questions if they are blindsided by the affirmative case. The priorities detailed above work both when you are prepared and when the case comes out of nowhere. If you have trouble following the case, the odds are that the judge will be disoriented as well. The audience might appreciate the direction provided by your questions about the case thesis and main points.

Prioritizing

After making sure you understand the crux of your opponent's advocacy and that you are arguing about the same thing, you can ask questions designed to garner admissions. We construct guidelines for your triage based on what area of Aristotle's rhetoric the questions target.

The topic areas you address in cross-examination should be Ethos, Pathos, Logos and Perspective, in that order. Why this order? During a speech, the most important goal is to sell the perspective of the case (i.e., the overall defense of, or attack on the resolution). To support this goal, a logical case must be presented. But logic is important only insofar as it leads to the acceptance of the overall perspective. Emotion is the psychological engine that makes the logical vehicle run. Ethos is the vital prerequisite factor for the acceptance of the entire case. If the speaker lacks Ethos, the audience is unlikely to accept anything being advocated. If the speaker has Ethos, the audience is likely to listen to the rest of the argument with sympathy or at least attentive neutrality.[31]

The challenge is that you cannot argue in favor of your own Ethos. I cannot tell you to believe me because I *told* you to believe me. In a speech, therefore, Ethos is most properly put at a low priority. It is vital to demonstrate Ethos, but it is not a high priority for speeches. Cross-examination, however, unlike a speech, does not lend itself to an uninterrupted and protracted development of a case perspective or of the logic underlying it. Ethos, rather, is the most visible element with the emotional impact of the questions and answers running a close second.

Note that it is quite possible to pursue more than one rhetorical goal at a time. You may design questions that target your opponent's Pathos *and* Logos or Ethos *and* Pathos. Also, once you start a line of questioning, it is more important to sustain it to its conclusion than to satisfy any sort of rhetorical priorities. Avoid becoming wedded to any particular goal. If the question starts at the Ethos level and becomes a Logos discussion through the witness's responses, take the cross-examination there, especially if you are winning the point.

As you triage your questions, keep in mind that you can build on your partner's cross-examination. There is no need to reintroduce questions that have already been answered. If your partner strongly targeted Ethos,

---

[31] Cirlin, *supra*, at p. 9.

you might begin your cross-examination on Pathos questions. Listen to what your partner has done and work as a team.

Questioning Ethos

Does your opponent lack confidence, competence or knowledge about the subject? If you sense any weaknesses here, it may be possible to capitalize on his lack of Ethos. You want to ask questions that will provoke the other speaker without hurting your own Ethos—and while raising your own credibility to create a contrast. Generally these questions are about standards, thresholds and criteria for evaluating arguments. For example:

> *Q: Should Congress be concerned with the General Welfare?*
>
> *Q: How high is a just tax rate?*
>
> *Q: Is your criterion the highest value in the round?*
>
> *Q: You argued that schools were closing because of the harms in the status quo. How many schools would have to close as a result of the affirmative plan to justify a negative ballot?*
>
> *Q: If your plan raises the unemployment rate by 5%, is it still worth voting affirmative?*

Questioning Pathos

Is the opposition's Pathos weak? Are any of her arguments particularly foolish, badly presented, based on objectionable premises or totally and utterly ghastly? Has she presented arguments that don't feel right at a gut level? Did she drop an emotionally poignant argument? Is she not taking care of those she hurt, or is she discounting an important value? If so, this is the time to broach Pathos arguments. Examples include:

> *Q: How much is a human life worth?*
>
> *Q: Does your plan contain any provisions for those it displaces?*
>
> *Q: Did you respond to Harm 2, that birth defects are devastating communities that use chlorpyrifos?*

Questioning Logos

If there's one thing debaters learn with relative ease, it's that there is no unassailable position. There will always be *some* available argument. Therefore, this category of questions is where you set up your advocacy, phrase hypothetical questions and ask about the logic employed by your opponent. Examples of Logos questions include:

> *Q: Ten people are in a room. One of them will kill 2 million people if he escapes. But the other nine are innocent. Is it OK to kill all 10?*
>
> *Q: Is all life valued equally, or do we consider some lives differently?*
>
> *Q: Do you pay taxes?*

Questioning Perspective

The final category is the perspective employed by the opposing team. *Perspective* means the general philosophy that motivates the attitudes exhibited by your opponent. It could be something explicit—like a resolutional analysis—or it may be a subtle attitude or theme that permeates the advocacy. There is rarely any reason to approach this in cross-examination (this rhetorical element is much better suited to the rebuttals), but if there is a major flaw in your opponent's perspective worth exploiting, you may ask a question here. You may also resort to these questions if you can't think of anything to ask about on the other three levels. Your goal is to make your position look rosy and your opponent's look harsh, out of touch or just plain wrong. Examples include:

> *Q's: Your case has focused on the cost of subsidies. I want to look at farmers. How many farmers are there in the United States? How much do they produce? Are they considered a beneficial part of the economy?*
>
> *Q's: What happens to a deported immigrant? Does he lose his job? What happens to his family? If he has children in school, what happens to his children's education? Is that guaranteed in his country of origin?*
>
> *Q's: Your case alters our Native American reservation system, correct? Do we have an obligation under treaties? What role do treaties play in the U.S. Constitution? What does Article VI have to say about treaties? Do you think we should generally keep our promises?*

The process of writing a cross-examination tree will feel a little odd to you when you first get started. You will have to put yourself mentally in a round and imagine how your opponent will answer your questions. You will have to work in the solitude of your home, developing trees, practicing triage and categorizing questions by their rhetorical element before you are able to use this strategy fluidly.

But I think you will come to find that it is much more intuitive than many other methods of organization, and that it is much less taxing than memorization and contingency planning. The end result for my students has been a marked improvement in cross-examination ability. Implementing triage, trees and prioritization will be similarly effective for you.

Team-Policy Debaters in an outround at the National Championship in 2009

CHAPTER **5**

Examining the Examiner

"Any time you have an individual who is very confident in their abilities to persuade, there can be a rude awakening under cross-examination." —Catherine Crier

The examiner starts cross-examination in control. When the examiner wants to ask a question, cut off the witness, or do anything else that demonstrates his authority, he is given substantial leeway, as long the control is exerted politely. A judge may penalize examiners for failing to give the witness proper respect but will generally recognize their inherent authority to direct the conversation's flow.

But the mere fact that you start with the authority does not mean you'll still have it after three minutes. Firmly grasping the examiner's keys will help you build your credibility through the cross-examination period while ensuring that the witness loses ground.

Concentrate Your Fire

Scattershot argument is ineffective. It gives the impression of weakness and desperation, and it insults the intelligence of the judge. Roman rhetorician Quintilian said 2,000 years ago that "we must not always burden the judge with all the arguments we have discovered, since by doing so we shall at once bore him and render him less inclined to believe us."[32] So find a few areas to focus on and ask questions about them.

---

32 Quintilian. (1987). *Quintilian on the Teaching of Speaking and Writing: Translations From Books One, Two, and Ten of the Institution Oratoria.* (James J. Murphy). p. 147.

Before beginning your examination, you should have a very specific idea of where you want to go. Give considerable thought to what you will ask about. Discuss the areas of concentration with your partner and coach.

A corollary is that the examiner should not attempt to attack unassailable points. Some of the arguments in the witness's case are likely to be so well established that they are, for the purpose of cross-examination, irrefutable. An unsuccessful attack on them will only serve to highlight their strength. Focus on the points you think you can carry, and remember that it is always better to *sit* than to *assist* your opponent.

Hone Your Questions

Because you write down many of your questions and pre-script your trees, you can put some effort into making sure the questions limit the scope of potential answers and are tightly phrased. Wherever possible, ask questions that permit only a yes or no answer. Never ask open-ended questions, questions that begin with "why" or that ask the witness to explain. Hone your inquiry and keep your questions short. Leave out elliptical clauses, qualifying phrases, asides, irrelevancies, jokes and historical references. Go for the jugular.

Each query should contemplate only one thought. Compound questions should be divided into two or more simple questions. "Will corruption keep companies from investing in Venezuela and did you read evidence for that?" should be two questions, not one. If you want a usable admission, you need to start with a usable question. Hone your questions until they're ready for the rigors of cross-examination.

Think

Good cross-examination is the product of lengthy thought. The best lines of questioning might be born to the parents of sudden inspiration, but they're improved through steady mulling and frequent revisiting. As Quintilian said, "Undoubtedly ... the best method for correction is to lay by for a time what we have written, so that we may return to it after an interval as if it were something new to us, and written by another, lest our writings like newborn infants compel us to fix our affections on them."[33]

Keep the mental fires burning after you finish your first draft of a line of questioning. Stoke those fires by talking about your questions with debaters in your club and with your coaches and parents. Continue to read about and research the topic. As you keep working, you are sure to uncover new angles and routines.

Establish an Early Tone

The first five questions of your cross-examination set a tone for the entire three minutes. If you start with open-ended, undisciplined questions, let the witness wander around the answer or do not exert your authority early, you will be hard-pressed to earn it later. If the witness is allowed to win some confidence by getting away with a waffled response or half-answer or by winning an early exchange, you may find yourself fighting uphill for the duration of the cross-examination.

Where possible, start with a pre-scripted routine and tightly worded questions. Watch to see if the witness misinterprets a question to be *almost* what you asked. Point out the deficiency of the answer or rephrase your question as necessary. If the witness's misinterpretation is particularly egregious, you can simply repeat the question exactly as you originally asked it. (Be careful with this particular tactic: It puts the most emphasis on the witness's non-answer, but it can be regarded as overly confrontational.)

Have confidence in your questions. Do not back down simply because the witness is evasive or unresponsive. Push until you get the answer to the question *you* asked, not the question the witness wants to answer. If you establish an early tone and enforce answers powerfully, you will be in control throughout the cross-examination.

---

[33] Ibid.

Target Speech Content

Traditionally, cross-examination questions must focus primarily on arguments developed in the witness's speech. Indeed, arguments introduced and responses made in that constructive deserve priority. However, questions about arguments made by the witness's partner or matters that are clearly relevant to the topic may also be reasonable. Judges will not stop you if you ask an off-topic question, but you may begin to look unreasonable, and you allow the witness to credibly shrug and say, "I don't know."

Targeting speech content is especially important as it regards questions about your case and arguments. I observed the following exchange:

> *Q: I presented a disadvantage about environmental devastation, correct?*
>
> *A: [Consulting notes] I believe that was your second disadvantage.*
>
> *Q: Right. Do you agree that regulatory influences reduce pollution?*
>
> *A: That was the internal link in your disadvantage, I think. If you want to demonstrate that, you can try. My response is that I'm not sure and that it really doesn't matter because of the disadvantage answers I presented in my speech.*

The witness looked credible refusing to answer the question, because the query regarded the *examiner's* argument. Had the witness introduced evidence that regulatory influences reduce pollution and used that position as a disadvantage answer, his non-response would not have been reasonable. Because the questions had nothing to do with his arguments and case, he was justified in refusing to answer. Do not allow witnesses to escape your questions so easily; make sure your queries target speech content.

Build a Dog Kennel

Have you ever built a dog kennel? When I was 10 years old, our family adopted two puppies from an animal shelter. At first they were so small and vulnerable that we kept them in a laundry basket in our utility room. But as Oreo and Milou grew, they soon required new lodgings. That's when I was called on to help my father and some friends build a chain-link kennel.

I don't know what image is called to mind when *you* ponder dog kennels, but back then I thought we would plop some fence into the ground and call it complete. My father, who had some experience with dogs and knew their tendency to dig and escape, had more elaborate plans. We dug a ditch, inserted poles and poured cement. After hours of work, our project looked nothing like a kennel. I wondered if we had made some colossal mistake—until we stretched the fence, transforming our circled collection of posts into an escape-proof kennel.

Each step in the building process required action that had no obvious link to the end result. A casual observer would not have regarded our cement outline as a kennel in the making. The steel poles sticking out of the ground looked more like an alien shrine than a home for dogs. But each step had its own purpose, and together those steps led to a cozy confinement.

When you design a line of questioning it needs to be both escape proof and ambiguous. The witness should not have a firm idea of where you're going or they will head you off. So build a dog kennel by trapping your opponent into a particular position before turning up the heat.

Loop Important Questions

A great way to emphasize the posts of the dog kennel is by looping important questions. This means that you will repeat important parts of the witness's responses to provide greater emphasis.

> *Q: You argued in your case that the lack of health insurance was a problem, correct?*
>
> *A: I said that the status quo is working to provide alternatives to those without insurance and—*
>
> *Q: But is lack of insurance a problem?*
>
> *A: For those who do not have insurance, it's a serious problem.*
>
> *Q: A serious problem. What is the impact on those without coverage who become seriously ill?*
>
> *A: Well, it can be devastating.*
>
> *Q: Devastating—a serious problem and devastating. Thanks.*

Looped questions become boring fast and are not for every cross-examination and certainly not every question. But when you want to draw attention to powerful language used by the witness or emphasize a key post in your dog kennel, they can be very effective.

Use Summary Phrases

With witnesses who enjoy extemporizing and fluffy pontification, it is important to assert control over the flow and direction of the cross-examination. An excellent way of doing this is to incorporate summary phrases into your questions. Summarize the witness's response to the previous question before beginning the next. Borrowing an example from Austin J. Freeley:

> *Q: You claim industry will move to escape environmental controls?*
>
> *A: Right. They certainly will.*
>
> *Q: Would you please read that card? I think it was the—*
>
> *A: State Street Report. "When faced with unreasonably high taxes and excessive regulation, industry will give serious consideration to their option to move to a location that offers a more favorable business climate."*
>
> *Q: That specifically says a combination of high taxes and unreasonable regulations, doesn't it?*
>
> *A: Well, yes, but I think the focus is—*
>
> *Q: Does the evidence say that any industry moved because of environmental regulations alone?*
>
> *A: Um, no, I don't think so. Not in this report, but environmental controls are part of it.*
>
> *Q: Does the State Street Report specifically mention environmental controls?*
>
> *A: It cites "unreasonable regulations" and many of the—*
>
> Q: *[Using summary phrase]* No mention of environmental controls. Thank you. *And it said industry would consider moving, didn't it?*
>
> *A: Yes, and they have moved.*
>
> *Q: Does your evidence say so?*

A: Well, no, not this evidence. We have other evidence that my partner will read—

Q: We'll be looking for that in her speech. [Using summary phrase] But so far there is no evidence of industry moving; no evidence about environmental controls. Thank you.[34]

Summary phrases draw the judge's attention to the admission when the admission becomes clouded by a dodging witness.

Keep Your Questions Tight

When phrasing a question, use the most precise language possible. Open-ended or broadly worded queries allow the witness leeway to orate rather then just answer your question. By focusing your query, you make a wayward response unreasonable. Instead of asking, "What are the goals of NATO?" ask, "Is the principal goal of NATO to act as a peacekeeping force?" Don't ask, "Why is the Internet untaxed?" ask, "Is the purpose of a tax-free Internet to facilitate the free flow of information globally?"

If you make a mistake and ask an open-ended question, rephrase it as quickly as is reasonable. The follow-up question should be specific where the first one failed.

Q: What are the goals of NATO?

A: When NATO was first established there were several goals including keeping the former Soviet Union in check, coordinating military activities of the north Atlantic—

Q: Sure, but is the principal goal of NATO today to act as a peacekeeping force?

Questions that start with "Do you think," "Can you explain" or "Why" invite the respondent to give the best possible reasons for their position. Avoid these introductions to keep your questions focused. Keeping your questions tight ensures that the witness will only answer the questions you intend to ask.

---

[34] Freeley, Austin J. and Steinberg, David L. (2008). *Argumentation and Debate.* (Wadsworth).

Ask Questions Syllogistically

If you've never studied logic, you may be surprised to learn—like the man who was astounded to discover that he had been speaking prose all his life[35]—that you've been using syllogistic reasoning all along. Logic is an intrinsic element of human reasoning. Because we all have the capacity to think logically, logic is an integral part of argumentation. The most rigorous and, by extension, persuasive form of logic is syllogistic reasoning. To put an argument into a syllogism is to strip it bare for logical inspection. It allows you to see where the weak points are, if, of course, the argument has any.[36]

Absolute arguments can be expressed syllogistically:

> **Major Premise**: All X is Y.
>
> **Minor Premise**: This case is X.
>
> **Conclusion**: This case is Y.

If the major premise (the broad rule) and the minor premise (the facts invoking that rule) are true, the conclusion follows inevitably. The examiner's advantage is knowledge of the conclusion. Ask questions proving the premises and you will have won the conclusion. The witness can only guess what end result the premises are designed to produce. He will therefore answer questions about the premises blindly.

Say you have a politics disadvantage against a case that would amend America's prescription drug plan for seniors. Your syllogism might look like this:

> **Major Premise**: Only expanding protections for America's seniors will serve the policy objectives of the current Congress.
>
> **Minor Premise**: The affirmative plan would increase seniors' insurance premiums by $2,000/year.

---

35 Molière, Jean-Baptiste Poquelin. (1670). *Le Bourgeois Gentilhomme.* (Henry Holt; New York).

36 Frank, Jerome. (1949). *Courts on Trial*. pp. 184-185.

> **Conclusion**: The affirmative plan contradicts the policy objectives of the current Congress.

If you were to ask the witness whether his plan "contradicts the policy objectives of the current Congress," you would hear a quick "of course not." But by asking questions syllogistically, you will get a very different outcome:

> *Q: Is the current Congress concerned at all about seniors?*
>
> *A: Sure.*
>
> *Q: Is the current Congress trying to expand protections for American seniors?*
>
> *A: Yes.*
>
> *Q: Would your plan increase insurance premiums for seniors?*
>
> *A: By about $2,000 per year, yes.*

It takes work to convert arguments into syllogisms and you will want to practice argument deconstruction. Can you identify the major and minor premises? Does the conclusion follow? Once you have pared an argument down to its most basic elements, you will be able to elicit damaging admissions without ever asking about the conclusion directly.

Imply the Major Premise

Some of walls of your dog kennel are already built and do not need to be reestablished in cross-examination. In logical terms, the major premise is implied. Aristotle termed the resulting statement an "enthymeme"—simply a syllogism with an implied major premise. For example:

> **Implied Major Premise:** Effective enforcement of new laws requires new funding.
>
> **Minor Premise:** The affirmative allocates no new funding for enforcement of its new law.
>
> **Conclusion:** The new law will not be effectively enforced.

Enthymemes are useful when asking a question about the major premise may tip off the witness about the direction of your questions. If you feel confident that you can demonstrate a key premise in your syllogism (or if the premise is clearly articulated in your opponent's harms, plan, value, etc.), do not ask about the major premise and keep your routine under the witness's radar.

Signpost

When debaters communicate, they take great pains to incorporate signposts into their speaking. They regularly identify where they are in the argument to make sure the judge can keep tabs on the content. Take advantage of that effort during cross-examination by continuing to let the judge and your opponent know where you are. Instead of asking about the "Marshall '08" evidence, say, "Under solvency, you read a card from Marshall, correct?" The judge will be able to identify the source in question more easily, and you will be able to better apply the admission during your speech ("On solvency, I asked in cross-examination ...").

Peg

The cross-examination does not exist in a void, separate from the events it immediately follows or proceeds. Rather it comes directly after a constructive in order to allow for questions that stem from issues introduced in that speech. Effective examination takes advantage of this by pegging questions to the witness's earlier words, quoting him if possible, or having him reread salient evidence. Once you have identified the comment made during the speech, you are ready to ask a question about it. For example:

Q: Would you reread your evidence from Brookings under "Harm 1"?

A: Sure, the card from Henry Aaron?

Q: Yes.

A: "About 85% of Americans have health insurance. In general, it is good insurance. For two-thirds, it is privately managed."[37]

---

[37] Aaron, Henry J. (March 17, 2010). "Cricket, Rugby and U.S. Health Reform: Three Sports, in Increasing Order of Violence." *Brookings*. URL: http://www.brookings.edu/speeches/2009/1223_health_care_aaron.aspx ACCESSED: March 17, 2010.

Q: Aaron is saying that 15% of Americans don't have health insurance, correct?

Rather than asking whether your opponent has an answer to a particular argument (to which the answer will presumably be "Sure, let me elaborate"), ask if a response was presented during his speech.

Q: Did you respond during your speech to my third harm?

A: Which one was that again?

Q: Procedural injustice.

A: Oh, no. Not in this speech.

Taught early that you were listening to his speech, the witness will be more likely to agree with you and less likely to backtrack on his earlier statements for fear of getting caught. Pegging also reduces the risk that the witness will ramble through or extemporize the cross-examination, for fear of contradicting earlier statements. So when you face a recalcitrant witness, start pegging.

Prod

In their haste to be contradictory and argumentative, some witnesses will go against whatever they think the examiner is hunting. A slight current is all it takes to get them moving upstream. If you sense the witness is utilizing this knee jerk obstructionism, formulate questions that confuse the current.

Q: The Government Accountability Office is a credible source, correct?

A: Well, it is a government source, so there are concerns attendant to that—such as ties with K Street lobbyists or concern about political influence in its decision making—

An evasive witness will avoid a straight answer. So try this:

Q: Can we agree that the Government Accountability Office is a biased source?

A: Every source has some bias. I think the GAO has consistently shown that it reports accurate data and is generally immune from political influences.

Q: So you think the GAO is a credible source?

Trapped by his earlier position, the examiner is forced to agree. His filibustering caught up to him. If you sense the witness will push against you by reflex, set a trap by camouflaging your intent. Prod the witness by giving him something to push against.

Avoid Complicated Hypothetical Questions

Hypothetical questions, questions by analogy, and other lengthy and complicated questions are almost always a bad idea. I wish I had a nickel for every time a 20- to 30-second question targeting a common sense admission is met with a five-second punch line from the witness. And why shouldn't it be? Even the most stoic debater can find something funny to say in 30 seconds. One of my students was the witness in a cross-examination where the examiner spent the better part of a minute asking a question about obeying driving rules. He was trying to establish that it was generally a good idea to follow government-imposed standards to build a disadvantage against my debater's case. At the end of the elaborate setup, my student responded, "I really don't know; I don't have my driver's license."

Hypothetical questions introduce an imaginary scenario or circumstance and ask the witness to comment on what should happen or what is morally right. The purpose is to create a situation that is parallel to one found in the debate round, but that has, hopefully, a much more obvious answer. Once the witness has admitted to something in the hypothetical world, the examiner will extrapolate from the simple response criticism for the witness's real-world stance.

The problem with most hypothetical examples is that they tend to be either too arcane or too obvious. Arcane questions—ones who's connection with the round is too ambiguous or far-reaching to have utility—do not garner usable admissions. Obvious hypothetical questions—where the connection is so apparent that even the most inept witness will credibly avoid an admission—stir things up but rarely catch the big fish.

If you must ask a hypothetical question, make sure you have a clear purpose. Keep your setup short and make sure your sought answer is very reasonable. The explanation of your hypothetical question must be simple and clear. Prepare follow-up questions on the expectation that the witness will try to wriggle away.

Finally, unless you are very confident in the question and feel you have no better way to garner that admission, throw it away. Hypothetical questions rarely pay, get complicated quickly and often play to the witness's advantage. There is seldom good cause to risk your credibility with a hypothetical question. Prepare them carefully, ponder their application, consider using the example in a speech, but only if the hypothetical question is the only way to get what you want should you proceed with it in cross-examination.

Demand an Example

Witnesses make outlandish statements. Backed into a corner with more of their preplanned escape routes disappearing with each response, the desperate witness will say something that is completely unsupported. Clinging to a wild hope that you will be bluffed off a question or decide not to press further, the witness will say something you know cannot be true. In response, some examiners will look flustered, show surprise or incredulously ask, "Really?" But great examiners demand an example.

> *Q: Your case advocates removing all U.S. military presence from Japan, correct?*
>
> *A: Yes.*
>
> *Q: What function do U.S. troops currently perform in Japan?*
>
> *A: They work with the Self-Defense Forces in a number of capacities including maritime and ballistic missile, communications security and disaster response.*
>
> *Q: And you are claiming that if the troops are drawn down, Self-Defense Forces will step up to fill the void?*
>
> *A: Yes, Self-Defense Forces are able to perform all the tasks that—*
>
> *Q: As well as American troops?*
>
> *A: Absolutely.*
>
> *Q: So there is no functional difference in the training or performance of Japanese and American armed forces?*

A: No, not at all.

At this point, the examiner might easily become flustered. The examiner knows he doesn't have any evidence refuting the witness's assertion that Japanese and American troops are functionally equal and worries that letting two unequivocal denials lie unopposed will cripple his future arguments. The examiner doubts the veracity of the witness's last two responses and may even feel they are completely senseless. It is time to demand that illustration.

Q: Can you give me an example of when Japanese troops were demonstrated to be equal to their American counterparts?

A: Er ... I can't call any to mind. I might have one at the table—

Q: Can you give me an example of where a country experienced no increase in domestic crime rates after an American troop drawdown?

A: No, I can't.

Demanding an example subtly shifts the burden of proof to your opponent. When you simply ask questions, the witness may be able to credibly deny your position. When you demand examples, he has to come up with something to support his previous response. If he does not or cannot, the response is automatically suspect.

Most witnesses will not be able to produce an example when pressed. But if someone does, cross-examine it.

Q: Can you give me an example of where a troop drawdown did not disrupt the domestic military?

A: Sure, I think the Soviet Union's withdrawal from Afghanistan in 1988-89 was successful. Over 50,000 troops left and the domestic forces were able to easily assume control.

Q: That withdrawal occurred during a time of conflict, correct?

A: Yes.

Q: Are we at war with Japan?

A: No.

Q: Thanks. ... And in Afghanistan the Taliban eventually assumed control, correct?

A: Um ... yes.

It is much better to demand an example than to ask for evidence. Examiners who have reached the end of their rope sometimes say, "Do you have any evidence for that?" This brisk question lacks the persuasive or burden-shifting advantages of requesting an example and rarely yields dividends because judges are programmed to dismiss it. How many times have you observed a witness promise evidence only to never come through? When you demand an example, you foreclose the witness's chance to prey on the judge's forgetfulness. The example has to come quickly for the cross-examination to move on; it cannot wait for prep time.

When done correctly, everyone will see the witness's mental wheels spin. When no example is presented, know that you have successfully stolen credibility from him.

Establish a Threshold

Some affirmative cases have known disadvantages. Expanding social programs will increase the tax burden. Banning deep-sea fishing will hurt the fishing industry. Reneging on social security's promise will hurt seniors. Teams that run cases with known disadvantages hope they can persuade the judge that the pros outweigh the cons and that the policy change is a good idea overall.

As soon as you know the affirmative case admits a disadvantage, you can ask threshold questions in cross-examination. The goal of threshold questions is to impress the judge with the magnitude of the potential disadvantage or to get the witness to commit to a threshold you can prove they violate. When agriculture policy was the debate topic, the most common affirmative case in my state was to abolish federal farm subsidies. This case had a known and generally accepted disadvantage that some farmers would be forced out of business. A point of contention was just how many farmers would lose their livelihood. We devised an establish threshold line of questioning that went like this:

> *Q: How many farmers must go out of business after your plan is adopted in order for the judge to be justified in voting negative?*
>
> *A: It's more than a matter of numbers. We need to create a system that will sustain farming without burdening taxpayers. That's the—*

> *Q: So if a million farms go out of business, the judge should still vote affirmative?*
>
> *This is over half of the roughly 1.9 million farms identified in the U.S. Census.*
>
> *A: That wouldn't happen. Under our plan—*
>
> *Q: Hypothetically. If a million farms went out of business should the judge vote negative?*
>
> *A: Hypothetically, um, sure, if a million farms went under, the judge shouldn't vote for that plan.*

The witness has now committed to a threshold, backtracking on his earlier comment that "it's more than a matter of numbers."

> *Q: How about 100? If 100 farms go out of business, should the judge vote negative?*
>
> *A: No, our advantages outweigh that.*
>
> *Q: 10,000?*
>
> *A: Still the same. The—*
>
> *Q: What about 100,000?*
>
> *A: [Pause] That gets to a harder calculus—and again, with private insurance and non-subsidy protections, the real bankruptcy rate will be nowhere near that—but, OK, sure.*
>
> *Q: If 100,000 farmers go out of business, the judge should vote negative. Thank you.*

It doesn't matter where the threshold is set. If the witness agrees to a threshold that you can demonstrate their case will exceed, you have a beautiful impact. You read the evidence that, say, 120,000 farmers will lose their jobs if a key subsidy is abolished and recite the admission above as evidence that this outweighs the affirmative's advantages. If the witness sets a very high threshold, argue that this standard reflects a mentality that undervalues the farmer's contribution. Use the cross-examination exchange as evidence of the affirmative's callousness. Even if the witness waffles by refusing to agree to a threshold, you have still won a usable admission. When you present the disadvantage, point out how the affirmative refused to acknowledge the problems caused by its plan in cross-examination. Keep in mind that if the judge feels your questions are reasonable, the waffling witness will lose credibility in the course of the exchange.

When you demand a threshold from your opponent, you pit yourself in a test of wills. The witness may try to waffle or complain that the standard you request is unreasonable. Push through until you have a threshold.

Elicit "I Don't Knows"

For the examiner, one of the most beautiful responses a witness can submit is a simple expression of ignorance. The vast majority of debate judges expect the witness to be familiar with the facts surrounding her case. Debating NATO, if the examiner asked a question like, "How many countries are in NATO?" or, "What year was the European Union established?" a short and succinct answer is reasonably expected.

The most common deployment of the "I don't know" is to cover for an answer the witness doesn't want to give. Say the witness is advocating NATO intervention in the genocide in Darfur and reads a piece of evidence from 1997 on the value of military intervention. The examiner wants to show that NATO has a failed history of peacekeeping and that more recent examples support the view that the organization is inept at halting wars. The "I don't know" might come out like this:

> *Q: Under solvency, you read a piece of evidence advocating military intervention in human rights crises, correct?*
>
> *A: Yes.*
>
> *Q: What was the date on that evidence?*
>
> *A: 1997*
>
> *Q: What year did NATO sponsor peacekeeping operations in Kosovo?*
>
> *A: Um. I don't know.*

The witness is unwilling to admit that her evidence is before the Kosovo intervention which occurred in 1999 and she chooses to deploy the "I don't know" instead. As an aside, the examiner could have asked his last question first to better trap the witness. The date on some solvency evidence is easier to verify than the witness's knowledge about events in Kosovo.

The value of an "I don't know" response for the examiner is that it disqualifies the witness's credibility. If the witness is unsure of an important fact and fails to provide a credible reason for the lack of knowledge, why should the judge pay attention to her position? The witness bleeds Ethos when she doesn't know something the judge thinks she should. The information you seek should reasonably be known by the witness (i.e., widely known general knowledge or facts obviously related to the topic or case). When you elicit a reasonable "I don't know," don't smile or act victorious. Treat it like any other admission and move on to your next line of questions.

Split Partners

In most cross-examination debate formats, the first affirmative speaker is cross-examined by the second negative and the second affirmative by the first negative. The division of labor on most negative teams divides case and off-case arguments between the first and second negative, respectively. The result is that each speaker asks cross-examination questions about the arguments they will run next. Because of how pervasive splitting the negative has become in modern forensics, first and second affirmative speakers will develop expert skill at answering questions about particular elements of their case. When negative speakers set up their own arguments, they charge the mouth of the cannon by directing questions to the speakers most prepared to answer them.

The solution is simple: Swap questions with your partner. Ask your case routines when the first affirmative is the witness and your off-case lines when the second affirmative answers questions. This strategy requires some work beforehand to make sure both partners understand the goal of each routine and may necessitate you swapping arguments with your partner as well, but it can be devilishly effective. Unless the affirmative is exceptionally prepared, the witness will be less prepared and you will elicit more admissions than if you asked your questions of the more prepared speaker.

"Thank You"

I maintain that "thank you" is the most powerful expression in the English language. No subject line is more likely to get someone to open an e-mail than "Thank You," and no phrase elicits more smiles in daily conversation. We like the idea that we did something good and are always encouraged by gratitude. Because *thank you* is such a friendly expression, it works very well when you need to cut off your opponent.

When the witness has wondered too far from the call of your question or has answered your question and is starting to elaborate, say, "Thank you, that gives me enough information," or, "Thank you, that makes your position clear," or, simply, "Thank you." Expressing gratitude is your first line of defense against a rambling witness.

Do Not Argue

Sometimes a witness will have a beef with something trivial. Perhaps your word choice riles him or he doesn't like your phrasing. In such cases, the following impasse is common:

Q: Did that incident cause a "complete rupture"?

A: No, I wouldn't describe it that way.

Q: Are you saying that everything about the policy was just fine?

A: Well, I would not call it a complete rupture.

Q: The contractors haven't gotten any more orders, have they?

A: Not so far.

Q: Isn't that a rupture?

A: I hope it isn't.

Q: Does your research suggest there will be future orders?

A: The research is inconclusive and—

Q: So no new orders and you still say there hasn't been a complete rupture?

A: I just wouldn't use those words.

Q: Why not?

> *A: It seems to me that a complete rupture means that things are over forever.*
>
> *Q: The business relationship has never been restarted, correct?*
>
> *A: Not as of today.*
>
> *Q: So it really was a complete rupture, wasn't it?*

It is almost always a mistake to argue with a witness. When you ask a question, you have a reasonable assumption that it will be answered. You can at least rely on the witness to phrase their response as an answer. When you argue with the witness, you don't know what he's going to say. You cede the examiner's high ground as soon as you take off the interrogator's hat and put on the boxing gloves.

In this case, the examiner has become enamored with a particular word choice and is determined to defend it, even as it gradually becomes more unreasonable. The additional questions about a "complete rupture" are getting her nowhere. Some observers might say the examiner is impeding her own cross-examination by making the witness more tense and unhelpful, rather than cooperative and forthcoming. Consider the following change:

> *Q: Did that incident cause a "complete rupture"?*
>
> *A: No, I wouldn't describe it that way.*
>
> *Q: How would you describe it?*
>
> *A: I guess ... I guess I'd call it a "serious breakdown."*
>
> *Q: That makes sense. What were the immediate consequences of this serious breakdown?*

By adopting the witness's own terminology, the examiner is more likely to obtain useful information. She surrendered her original verbiage, but the reward will be worth the cost. Remember that only the next question matters, the last one is already gone. So keep asking questions, not picking fights.

Expose, Yes; Explain, No

Hardball's Chris Matthews asks tough questions, but he would be a terrible cross-examiner. Like most journalistic reporters, Matthews researches contradictions, trackbacks and inaccuracies made by his interviewees. Equipped with his guest's previous statements and written comments, Matthews is ready to interrogate. But, ultimately, his goal is to give his subject a chance to respond. He wants an apparent contradiction explained or trackback justified. He poses pointed questions to make *Hardball* a compelling news digest, not to expose weakness in his interviewees.

As the examiner, you want no explanation. Elucidation is for rebuttal. The goal of your questions is simply to outline and expose a weakness. An admission is made when the posts of the dog kennel are outlined, not necessarily when they are fully articulated. The skilled examiner, therefore, will never ask, "Isn't this a contradiction?" or, "Can you explain this?" Chris Matthews might, because the purpose of his interviews is to explain. You will not, because the purpose of your questions is to expose.

Stop at the Penultimate Question

It is not hard to understand, at least at an intellectual level, the lurking danger inherent in one question too many. Having painstakingly trapped a witness in an apparent contradiction or equivocation, the overeager examiner is not content to leave the finishing touch for his speech. Instead, he will attempt to deliver the *coup de grace*, asking the ultimate question—only to be painfully surprised by the witness's artful explanation.

A story is told about a young Abraham Lincoln, who was representing a defendant charged with biting off another man's nose. The prosecution called a single witness who testified that Lincoln's client had indeed done the atrocious deed. On cross-examination, Lincoln set out to show that the witness could not have seen all that he claimed.[38]

> *Q: The two men were fighting in the middle of a field?*
>
> *A: Yes.*
>
> *Q: You were bird-watching at the time?*

---

[38] Younger, Irving. *The Ten Commandments of Cross Examination.* (National Institute for Trial Advocacy).

A: True.

Q: Weren't the birds in the trees?

A: They were.

Q: And the trees were on the edge of the field?

A: That is right.

Q: So you were looking away from the middle of the field?

A: I was.

So far, Lincoln has performed a textbook cross-examination. He has demonstrated that the witness's head was turned away from the action. Rather than looking at the fight, he was directing his attention to the birds at the periphery of the field. Stop! Mission accomplished! Go no farther! But, no, Lincoln made the fatal error of asking another question.

Q: Then how can you say that you saw my client bite off the other man's nose?

A: Because I saw him spit it out.

The extra question must never be asked; it leads only to catastrophe. Picture a cross-examination as a sword fight by a cliff with the examiner pushing the witness back with every stroke of his saber. The examiner should only press until the witness is at the cliff's edge. If he issues one more blow at the precipice, both will fall over. The examiner should leave the witness in a precarious position until his speech, when he can deliver the fatal blow without losing his own footing. You should never give the witness the chance to explain an apparent contradiction or otherwise sneak out of the kennel's confines.

Q: You support intervention in genocide situations because genocide is a war crime, correct?

A: Yes, the Geneva Convention explicitly prohibits the kind of activity we see in Darfur.

Q: So the law should be upheld?

A: Yes.

Q: Always?

A: Yes.

> *Q: Was NATO intervention in Kosovo in 1999 legal or illegal by the standards of the time?*
>
> *A: The NATO intervention in Kosovo was illegal by the standards of the time.*

Stop! The admission has been garnered. The issue has been exposed. The penultimate question has been asked. Any more questions would guild the lily. *Stop!*

> *Q: So doesn't intervention contradict your goal of upholding the law?*
>
> *A: Not at all, the United Nations ruled that the intervention was legal a year after Kosovo. Our plan follows the same path that the U.N. said was justified.*

The examiner's last question destroyed the momentum of an otherwise powerful line of questioning. Of course the witness feels that intervention is legal. That is her case! The time to point out the contradiction is during your speech when she cannot contradict you. Once you have the speaker in a tight spot, leave her there and go to another line of questioning.

Students often ask how to tell when they are nearing the precipice. While experience and practice are the only guaranteed ways of learning how to avoid the one-question-too-many pitfall, a good rule of thumb is to stop immediately before you might otherwise ask, "Can you explain this?" or, "Isn't there a contradiction here?" As soon as the point is apparent and clear enough that you can quickly and neatly shut the dog kennel door in your rebuttal, move on.

Find the Weak Point

The most common question posed by students about the examiner is where to start attacking. This question is especially routine with respect to unexpected affirmative cases. Debaters want to know what to ask when they have never before prepared for that affirmative plan. They want to know what parts of a case are most vulnerable to probing and inspection. While flaws vary from case to case, there are a few tips to catching the major exploitable weaknesses of the other side's argument.

Shifts in advocacy

When your opponents alter their position, the best time to point out the shift is in cross-examination. One of my students faced an affirmative running a very broad net-benefits criterion. In response, he introduced a counter-criterion that limited the scope of the round. In counter-response, the affirmative team tried to demonstrate how net benefits can be useful as a limit by narrowing the focus of its criterion. My student caught the advocacy shift in cross-examination.

> *Q: In your case, your partner presented a criterion of net benefits, correct?*
>
> *A: Yes.*
>
> *Q: How did he define net benefits?*
>
> *A: It's—as a comparative advantage, weighing the disadvantages vs. the advantages.*
>
> *Q: OK. Is any one issue weighed more significantly than another?*
>
> *A: No, not in net benefits.*
>
> *Q: And that's your criterion for the round, correct?*
>
> *A: Yes.*
>
> *Q: In your speech you introduced a "lens" of life, correct?*
>
> *A: Yes.*
>
> *Q: Did you introduce this lens in the 1AC with net benefits or in your speech?*
>
> *A: In the 2AC—in my speech.*
>
> *Q: And you said that this lens acts as a focus for the criterion—*
>
> *A: Yes—*
>
> *Q: To help evaluate the round?*
>
> *A: That's correct.*

This line of questioning outlines the shift for the judge. The judge can see clearly how the team's position on the criterion moved from the 1AC to the 2AC. All the negative team needs to do to defeat the criterion is reference the shift and this admission during the negative block.

Contradictions

Renowned (and reviled) tobacco lobbyist Nick Naylor tells us that "the beauty of argument is, if you argue correctly, you're never wrong." Naylor makes a good point in that the fog of argumentation often allows a speaker to hide behind hypocrisy, but he doesn't account for cross-examination. An argument *can* be wrong and it often demonstrates its flaw through contradiction.

A contradiction exists wherever a team backtracks over an earlier position. Because of the complexity of the issues contemplated by debate, many teams contradict themselves inadvertently. Internal consistency is an imperative element of sound argumentation, so demonstrating that an argument contradicts itself can be enough to win.

I was debating negative against an affirmative case that strove to both revive and control the African elephant population. The affirmative quoted evidence from conservation experts in Kenya, where elephant populations were severely endangered, and Zimbabwe, where legislative efforts to promote population growth have been so effective that citizens often regard elephants as pests, especially when they trample crops and cause property damage. In cross-examination, I exploited the ambiguity in the affirmative's presentation (they did not distinguish between the two countries) to ask the following:

> *Q: Under your Reasons for Change, you talked about the endangered African elephant population, correct?*
>
> *A: Yes.*
>
> *Q: And that's a significant issue, this elephant population crisis?*
>
> *A: Yes, we quoted evidence from the International Fund for Animal Welfare about how poachers have decimated elephant populations.*
>
> *Q: That evidence said that current population levels are far below where they were a decade ago, right?*
>
> *A: Yes.*
>
> *Q: How much of a problem was property damage by elephants a decade ago?*
>
> *A: My evidence was more recent, so I'm not sure.*
>
> *Q: But it was a big issue?*

A: I assume so, yes.

Q: So because of the decline in the elephant populations, it must not be as big of an issue today.

A: No, my evidence said it's a major issue for farmers and villagers, especially in rural areas.

Q: Oh, it is a big issue?

A: Yes.

Q: These last remaining elephants must be very good at what they do. Thank you.

Equivocation on terms

Even though affirmatives devote a minute or more of their first constructive to defining the key terms in the debate, equivocation, or shifting definitions, is common. Definitions may become inconvenient and debaters will slip into utilizing a new definition, often one that is terribly inconsistent with the one introduced at the beginning. This problem is especially pronounced in values debate where the outcome of a round can hinge on the definition of a key term. In some rounds, a miscommunication derails an entire argument and needs to be brought back around in cross-examination.

The most egregious example of equivocation caught in cross-examination that I can recall occurred during my freshman year. The affirmative team was one of the best in the state (one of the debaters is now an Ivy League law graduate, the other is a nationally recognized social issue advocate) and my partner and I were pumped to take them down. I understood the affirmative case to be dealing with bioterrorism and constructed my negative around that understanding. I pulled out our bioterrorism brief and, my confidence rising, got ready to deliver the knockout punch. After eight minutes of bliss, I invited cross-examination:

Q: Hi, Cody, how are you doing?

A: Great, thanks.

Q: So, is our case dealing with bioterrorism or agroterrorism?

A: I thought it was bioterrorism ... if you look at your mandates. [I flipped through the affirmative's case and noticed my mistake] ... Well, it's actually more agroterrorism, now that I have it in front of me.

Q: So our case is dealing with agroterrorism?

A: [Weakly] Yes.

I learned two lessons in that debate round: First, listen closely to the affirmative's case. Second, cross-examination is a brutally effective time to point out equivocation errors. If you see that the other team is misinterpreting a key aspect of your case or is misusing an important term, ask about it in cross-examination.

Evidence specificity

Because of the importance of evidence to debate, especially in policy debate, many cross-examination questions center on the language particular authors use to describe their viewpoints. In their haste to be persuasive, some advocates brush over ambiguous language in their evidence. This is especially common when debaters present academic or legal research which generally use indefinite phraseology. The following is typical:

Q: To show your case's solvency, you quoted a case study from South America, correct?

A: Yes.

Q: Did that evidence say your plan might reduce government health expenditures, or that it would?

A: The card says that "if these reforms are implemented on a national level, they might likely reduce government health expenditures."

Q: So there is no guarantee.

Look out for conditional modifiers ("likely," "nearly"), limits on time frame ("The *status quo* will cost $50 billion over 30 years") and special circumstances in a case study. If you are suspicious of a piece of evidence but aren't sure that your opinion is actionable, ask to look at the card closer during your prep time.

Where a witness misrepresents the strength of his evidence, challenge his interpretation. When the witness tortures the author's intent, one of my favorite phrases is, "The evidence does not say that, does it?" This expression communicates the examiner's surprise at how the witness is choosing to use a particular card while giving them an out (reread the evidence). Never let evidence be misinterpreted in your cross-examination. If you know or are very sure that something is amiss with the other side's evidence, ask about it.

Source credibility

Although many of the sources used in academic debate are credible experts in their field, debaters sometimes resort to quoting bloggers, ill-qualified consumer advocates or unrefereed research journals. If you *know* that a source is not credible, you can probe your opponent's evidence in cross-examination. The caveat is that you must be very sure. You do not want to ask about an expert only to be flooded by an alphabet soup of qualifications, so be certain that the source is a flash in the pan before proceeding.

A creative way to expose a biased source is to ask about other comments made by that source. For instance, in a round where the affirmative wanted to abolish the Environmental Protection Agency and relied heavily on evidence from the Heritage Foundation, the following cross-examination question was appropriate:

> *Q: Can you name any EPA policy that the Heritage Foundation supports?*

Although there are probably EPA policies that the Heritage Foundation does support, the witness could name no such policy. This response created for the judge a very one-sided image of the Heritage Foundation. Instead of being an impartial policy think tank, the Foundation assumed the image of an EPA hatchet, out to cut down environmental policy at every turn.

Simply demonstrating that a source lacks credibility is not enough to defeat an argument. Points against an opponent's evidence weaken the argument, but you will need something else to defeat it altogether. Attacking evidence can be a great start, however, and evidence questions are best raised in cross-examination.

Omissions

Whether through strategy or error, debaters regularly drop arguments. In most judges' paradigms, a dropped argument no longer has weight in the round. Use cross-examination to politely point out that these arguments were dropped.

> *Q: Did you respond in your speech to Reason for Change 1?*
>
> *A: I answered generally to all the Reasons for Change.*
>
> *Q: But did you present a unique response to Reason for Change 1?*
>
> *A: No.*
>
> *Q: Did you respond to my first or second solvency points?*
>
> *A: No, I did not.*

You can ask, "What was your answer the Reason for Change?" but avoid asking the witness to respond to these arguments or demand whether or not they "have" a reply. Even if they did not present an argument in their speech, they will probably "have" something for you in cross-examination. So just ask whether the witness introduced a response during the speech.

Lack of specification

Similar to pointing out omissions, you can use cross-examination to draw the judge's attention to ambiguities in the affirmative's plan.

> *Q: Did you specify a funding source in your proposal?*
>
> *A: No specific funding source, no.*

If you are running a disadvantage linking to the affirmative's lack of funding specification, this question will draw the judge's attention and keep your opponent from trying to specify a funding source later.

Note that while these questions *clarify* an issue, they are not *clarification questions*. The witness is not given open license to pontificate on his funding source; he is asked whether one was specified. When asking clarifying questions, be sure to limit the witness's range of potential responses and feel free to cut him off when he begins to ramble. Renown debate coach Austin J. Freeley uses the following example:

Q: Your plan calls for placing a space station in orbit. What sort of an orbit will that be?

A: Geosynchronous. That way we will be able to—

Q: Thank you. That's what I wanted to know.[39]

This brief exchange clarified the affirmative's plan. The negative now knows that the affirmative is going to use a high orbit that will be more costly than a low orbit and will present more technical difficulties.

When evaluating questions to ask about the plan, look for:

1. Extra-topical mandates: These are any non-topical part of the plan. You can argue that advantages stemming from these mandates should not be considered since they are not arguments in favor of adopting the resolution.

Q: What does the resolution require?

A: It requires a change to agriculture policy.

Q: What is your second mandate?

A: It expands prison penalties and raises parole standards for pesticide violators.

Q: Prison penalties and parole standards. So you are changing prison penalties?

A: Yes—

Q: And parole standards?

A: Yes.

The negative will argue on rebuttal that any advantage related to expanded enforcement is extra-topical and should not be considered.

2. Additional required action: Any private, non-governmental or other government action that is required in order for the affirmative mandates to be realized. If private companies have to do something in order for the plan to work, there is a chance the plan will not be successful.

Q: Your plan will legalize DDT production in the United States, correct?

---

[39] Freeley and Steinberg, *supra*.

A: Yes.

Q: And you are doing this in order to allow for the production of DDT for use in Third World countries, right?

A: That's right, we have to stop the malaria epidemic.

Q: Under your plan, will the government produce DDT?

A: No, private companies will do the production.

Q: Where do you mandate that?

A: We don't mandate it; we anticipate that private companies will produce DDT once it is legal.

Q: Thank you.

3. Vague or ambiguous mandate: Any unclear, ambiguous or nebulous aspect of the affirmative plan can be explored in cross-examination. Vagueness is generally resolved by the agency of enforcement and can be an open door to abuse.

Q: Your mandate was to ban all public smoking, correct?

A: Yes.

Q: Did you define "public smoking" in your case?

A: No, we think that's pretty self-explanatory.

Q: Is smoking on private land in public view "public smoking"?

A: Er—

Q: How about smoking in a private vehicle while on government-owned land?

A: I'm not sure.

With the now-clarified (or muddied) plan before them, the negative can develop attacks targeting the specifics to which the affirmative has now committed. If the case is even more nebulous than before, the negative can impact the vagueness by arguing that the affirmative's agency of enforcement will abuse the broad discretion provided by the mandate.

Badger the Witness

My younger brother and his partner ran a case to route corruption out of the North Atlantic Treaty Organization. The thesis of the case was that NATO has no accountability mechanism and that the North Atlantic Council has a moral imperative to respond and provide such a mechanism. We worked to develop a ruinous cross-examination scheme, asking false front question after false front question.

1. Is corruption bad?
2. Is corruption immoral?
3. Do you support accountability?
4. Without accountability will corruption thrive?
5. Should a bank hire a known thief as a teller?

The answers to all of these questions are obvious. Corruption is bad staid by definition and most people's moral compasses don't allow for it. Accountability is something most people laud, at least in theory, and it is also the antidote to corruption. The hypothetical question about a thief as a bank teller is oxymoronic and similarly blatant. The questions prove their points easily, but if you stop and think about it, they don't prove the affirmative's point about NATO and corruption.

We put this routine at the beginning of cross-examinations with witnesses who had a reputation for being evasive. Whenever the witness tried to dodge the questions, the routine was devastating. Stubborn witnesses would either flop around wildly, trying to avoid answering the simple questions they were asked or hesitate mightily before giving the easy answer. One witness even went so far as to say that in principle corruption was good, accountability bad and that the two have no relation! If you think the witness will try to evade your questions, start badgering.

Pause With Power

A very important rhetorical skill that is tragically undervalued in modern debate is the pause. Pauses, though perfectly natural in everyday conversation, are lost to the rat-a-tat-tat of debate delivery. A strategic pause after an admission will emphasize whatever damaging comment you elicited from the witness. The still air allows the audience to ponder anything stated immediately before the silence. Pausing is like licking a stamp: Whatever was just said will be mailed right to your judge.

You will feel like jumping up and down while shouting "gotcha!" after executing a routine successfully. Good examiners exhibit more tact by inserting such comment as, "That's what I wanted to know," "Let's move on," or even the defiant, "We will definitely have something to say about that." The *best* reaction, however, to a witness's admission is a pause. Stand still, not saying a word, perhaps leafing through your notes absently or taking a slow breath. The cough of the grandparent in the third row, the muffled comment from the round next door and your opponent's glaring admission will all be highlighted by a 1- to 2-second pause.

But a pause does more than just dig at your opponent. It also reveals your control over the cross-examination. Your base communication impulse will drive you to exert your control more consciously by continuing to talk. But powerful communicators are not afraid of losing their podium or attention if they stop speaking for a few seconds. That's why novice or nervous speakers tend to speak quickly. A brief silence, in contrast, highlights your composure and control.

Think of the pause as a sizzle, like the sound of a thick-cut steak searing on an open grill. Your pause puts the witness closer to the fire and turns up the gas. The sizzle may only be audible to you, but it's there. And a demure silence emphasizes the sizzle much better than continued jabbering. As you pause, the admission will fill the room with its aroma.

A pause also prepares your audience for your next question. Rather than fruitless transitional verbiage, a brief pause gets listeners ready for what follows while allowing you to organize your thoughts. Next time you get an admission, pause. Enjoy the sizzling silence. And then start your next line of questioning.

Exercise Self-Control

Examiners need to maintain a poised control over their emotions, especially after the witness makes a damaging statement. Damaging answers are an examiner's fact of life. If you show by your face or posture that an answer hurts, or if you go sheepishly on to another subject, you draw the judge's attention to the response. An examiner who gulps, blushes and then, after allowing the answer its full lethal effect, moves forward, is not in control of the cross-examination.

It can similarly be very difficult to control your facial expression immediately after winning a key admission. When I was a freshman, the most common criticism of my cross-examination was that I was "sharkish." There are many ways of expressing over-aggressiveness or impoliteness, but judge after judge connected me with boneless water-dwellers. One of the coaches in our club, an expert in nonverbal communication, diagnosed the problem: Every time I won an admission, I would smile.

It's easy to do, of course. You know that an important point has been made and your impulse is to celebrate. You try to pause, but the corners of your lips turn up into a victorious grin. Hold back. Admissions should be met with sobriety and nonchalance. If you cannot remain expressionless, a slight lip purse is better than a sharkish smile.

End on a Zinger

When possible, always end your cross-examination on a strong point. If the other team takes prep time, your last line of questioning will echo between the judge's ears. If you have a set routine that consistently produces a zinging admission, employ it at the finish for maximum effect.[40]

When my partner and I ran an HMO reform case, we worked up the following line of questioning which almost always garnered the intended admission:

Q: What is the principal motivation behind the operation of a business?

A: To make money. Companies are motivated by profit.

Q: OK. Are insurance companies businesses?

A: Yes.

---

[40] Brown, Peter Megaree. (1987). *The Art of Questioning*. (Macmillan). pp. 43-44.

> *Q: Do insurance companies save money by not paying for health care?*
>
> *A: Yes.*
>
> *Q: Thank you. No further questions.*

The beauty of this line of questioning is that the first question contains the trap. While there is only one reasonable answer to the second and third questions, the first question affords myriad reasonable responses. Fortunately for us, witnesses tend to start waffling when they sense a trap. By putting the trap question first, we were able to get an easy, simple answer that then flowed naturally to an admission. A prepared witness might have answered the first question with, "To meet demand," or, "To provide a product or service," thereby hamstringing the line of questioning. But by placing this question at the beginning, we fooled the witness into committing to the admission. The damage was not apparent until the final question.

When the timer signals 30 seconds remaining, launch into your final prepared line of questioning. You can sit down happily once you have landed your last zinger.

Apply Admissions

Think of admissions garnered on cross-examination as your star evidence. They are from a source the opposing team cannot credibly indict (themselves), they were presented recently in front of the judge and were placed in the context of the issues in the debate round. No evidence is better than a cross-examination admission.

Why do so many debaters *not* use their admissions? There's actually no good answer for that. The majority of judges will not weigh cross-examination admissions in their decisions unless they are applied later in the round. So it's flat-out unfortunate that so many beautiful admission gems are lost because they're omitted from the rebuttals. Here's how you will avoid this pitfall:

During your prep time, compare your prepared lines of questioning to your flow (your notes about the round). Identify all the areas that you or your partner discussed in cross-examination and make a "CX" notation on your flow. When you deliver your rebuttal, take your cross-examination routines with you so you can clearly recount the events of cross-examination every time you see a "CX."

Think of the admission as the "support" element of a four-point refutation: 1) Identify your argument, 2) Explain it, 3) Support it with the cross-examination admission, 4) Impact the argument on the round. Instead of reading a source for your evidence, introduce the admission with a phrase like, "My opponent admitted in cross-examination," or, "In cross-examination we discovered." Always apply admissions. You do not want to have bullets left in your gun at the end of the shootout. You worked hard to earn the ammunition—pull the trigger.

CHAPTER **6**

Examining Poker for Cross-Ex Clues

I grew up with four competitive brothers who loved to challenge each other. Whether the sport was Ping-Pong, basketball or debate, we were always looking for outlets for our competitive drive. As academically minded youths, we would read whatever we could get our hands on to improve our game. My oldest brother, Ryan, for instance, learned some nasty Ping-Pong spins that made him king of the table for over a month. Research and practice were required to oust him from his throne.[41]

When we purchased play chips and discovered poker—a game of wagering and confidence—we continued our habit of investigation and preparation. Although there are many variants on the basic rules of poker, the essence of the game is that the players place bets on the relative strength of their hands against their opponents' hands. It's a game of imperfect information, meaning that you only know your own position and have little to no knowledge of your opponents' hands. After years of playing poker and debating, the strong connection between wagering and cross-examination was made clear.

I'll relay that connection to you in this chapter, but first, a caveat: Some people do not play poker (even absent its monetary component) for moral

---

[41] Charyn, Jerome. (2002). *Sizzling Chops and Devilish Spins: Ping-Pong and the Art of Staying Alive.* (Da Capo Press).

reasons. They are wary of the get-rich-quick mentality,[42] noting the dangers of loving money.[43] Others are reticent to become involved in a game that is, by all accounts, addictive. By some measures, 4% to 7% of casino gamblers are addicted to poker.[44] Many more are addicted to video poker or online gaming. Poker addiction destroys families and lives and is tragically avoidable. So while comparing cross-examination strategies to poker may be seen as an endorsement of the game, I want to make clear that I am not suggesting students play poker. Because it is a widely understood and intuitively easy game, poker is a superb pedagogical tool. And that's how I will use it here—strictly as a teaching mechanism. The lessons in this chapter can be learned without ever touching a poker chip or playing card.

Cross-Examination Winners and Losers

In cross-examination, each side wants to improve its own credibility while detracting from opponents'. You come into cross-examination with a stockpile of credibility. But at the end of it, the winning side will have experienced a net credibility gain. A net credibility loss means something went wrong.

Credibility is made up of a number of factors:

1. *Likeability*—how much the judge likes you
2. *Reasonableness*—how much the judge is willing to pay attention to you
3. *Sincerity*—how much the judge is empathetic toward you
4. *Trustworthiness*—how much the judge believes you
5. *Authority*—how much the judge thinks you know about the topic

The witness and the examiner both have credibility, although they are unlikely to have equal amounts. During cross-examination, credibility is

---

42 Proverbs 13:11

43 1 Timothy 6:10

44 Launch Poker. (March 14, 2005). Poker Addiction. URL: http://www.launchpoker.com/psychology/-poker-addiction-/ ACCESSED: February 22, 2010.

exchanged. Each question introduced by the examiner represents a wager. The examiner is putting some of his credibility behind a question. With each answer, the witness is choosing to wager a certain amount of credibility by challenging the question or not answering forthrightly or even withdrawing by making an admission. The witness and the examiner are betting over the outcome of a situation in the round. You know your value, your evidence, your plan and all your available arguments. Your opponent knows some of what you know, but not all. You will react to your opponent's moves in light of available knowledge.

Three factors play into the outcome of these credibility wagers: 1) The round situation, 2) What your opponent does, and 3) What you do. The round situation means the evidence and arguments that are presented before the cross-examination. Even though you only control one of the three factors in cross-examination, you can still use strategy and tactics to gain the upper hand. A win is the result of how you play the game, not necessarily having the best round position. In fact, cross-examination exchanges are regularly won by the party that does *not* begin the exchange with an upper hand on the issues.

In poker, the players have a set number of chips. These chips represent their ability to wager on a given hand during the course of the game. The players have knowledge of their own hands, but imperfect information about their opponents' positions. Just like cross-examination, a win is the result of how you play the game, not necessarily having the best round position.

Of all the many poker variations—five-card draw, seven-card stud, high-low split and countless others—it is probably Texas Hold'em that most closely resembles cross-examination, because it is based upon a combination of concealed information and publicly shared evidence. In Hold'em, each player must make the best possible five-card hand by using any combination of his own two "hole" cards and another five communal cards that are dealt face up for use by everyone. The hole cards are dealt first, followed by an initial round of betting. Then the first three community cards—called the "flop"—are dealt, followed by another round of betting. Next comes the fourth community card (the "turn"), more betting, then the final community card (the "river"), and one last betting round. As in cross-examination, most of the information (represented by the flop, turn, and river) is shared, and therefore equally available to everyone. The most important facts (the hole, or "pocket" cards), however, remain privately held, to be revealed or withheld as each player determines best.[45]

In a televised poker tournament, professional poker player Phil Hellmuth once took on a pocket pair of kings, one of the best starting hands in Hold'em, with a 2-7, widely considered to be the worst starting hand. Each community card dealt made Hellmuth's position worse. But his opponent was frightened by the professional's confident betting and ended up folding after calling several Hellmuth raises. It didn't matter that Hellmuth had terrible position. It mattered how he played that position. In the same way, a champion cross-examiner will be able to win credibility from his opponent, even when the cards don't fall his way.

Bet

A bet is an initial move. It is the act of placing some of your credibility behind a position. By virtue of the fact that you ask a question and, by extension, ask the judge to pay attention to your query, you wager credibility. In cross-examination, the examiner makes the initial move by asking the first question in a routine.

A poker player usually bets when he likes his position. If a player feels there is an advantage available, he will put out some chips. Likewise, the examiner should not gamble credibility unless there is a chance to improve his position. A bet in any other circumstance is a waste. If you feel you have a good line of questioning, go ahead and bet. Otherwise stay silent.

The first lesson for any poker player is that the bets you *don't* make are at least as important as the ones you do. Maybe more. Since you cannot possibly win every hand, it is essential to minimize your losses when you are dealt weak cards. It costs chips to play a hand and more chips the longer you stay in. Conversely, it saves chips to fold a bad hand as early as possible, and saves the most chips if you fold before calling a single bet. A common strategy, therefore, is to only bet when you hold a

---

[45] McManus, James. (2003). *Positively Fifth Street: Murderers, Cheetahs, and Binion's World Series of Poker*. (Farrar, Straus and Giroux).

"premium" hand, meaning one that grants you the best chance of winning.

Jurist and advocacy expert Peter Megargee Brown says that examiners pursue lines of questioning too often. Unless a question is reasonably calculated to garner a usable admission, it should not be asked.[46] Rather than presenting scattershot arguments, identify your premium arguments and press those. Put your credibility behind questions you feel will improve your overall position in the round. If you doubt your question, it probably should not be asked.

Control the Chaos

Like poker, cross-examination is a series of complex events. While poker has over 2.5 million possible hands, the myriad issues contemplated in a typical debate round may well exceed this level of intricacy. Fortunately, like poker, outcomes are highly sensitive to initial conditions. Of the millions of possible hands, only a handful will be possible by the time the turn and river cards are dealt. And the importance of every community card depends on the player's pocket cards. The best cards at the beginning of a hand are usually going to be the best at the end. As one poker maven observed, "The best way to control chaos is at the beginning of the event."[47]

The *beginning of the event* in debate is determined by the arguments you present. If you introduce contradictory or ambiguous arguments, you can expect trouble in cross-examination. If you equivocate on a key term or use some underhanded chicanery, cross-examination will be your judgment day. If you run an unreasonable case about an arcane issue, the skilled examiner will expose your lack of equanimity. Control the chaos by creating a favorable starting position and choosing defensible turf.

---

[46] Brown, Peter Megargee. (1987). *The Art of Questioning: Thirty Maxims of Cross-Examination.* (New York: Macmillan).

[47] Phillips, Larry W. (1999) *Zen and the Art of Poker: Timeless Secrets to Transform Your Game.* (Plume). p. 25.

Take a Peek at Your Opponent's Cards

Knowledge is power in almost every setting where power makes a difference, but seldom more than in poker and debate. In both pursuits, there is a premium on reliable information, as adversaries are constantly trying to spot each other's weaknesses.

If you get caught peeking at your opponent's cards in poker, you'll be ostracized, banned or arrested, depending on the stakes of the game. But in debate, where the facts of the round are analogous to the cards in poker, you can legally "look at your opponent's hand." This peek happens long before the tournament, in the comfort of your home or at the library. It happens when you read through entire articles on a subject instead of just skimming through for the card you want to cut. It happens when you conduct peripheral background research to become better acquainted with the topic. The more prepared you are for the round, the more likely it is that you will know something about the topic before your opponent does. This knowledge is just as powerful as getting a clandestine look at your opponent's cards.

Fold

Poker is an iterated game. Each hand is followed by another. A new poker player is quickly taught that folding or surrendering in a given hand is not bad. It is not an admission of defeat and does not mean you will lose the game. Expert poker players fold many more hands than they play. Depending on the strategy the player employs, some poker players will automatically fold as many as eight or nine out of 10 hands they are dealt.[48]

Folding simply means that the player forfeits the right to any chips wagered for that hand. There are many reasons a poker player might fold; he might be out of position, have a poor starting hand or be stranded by the community cards. But folding isn't giving up. It actually demonstrates a confidence in the *next* hand. It says, "Even though I know

---

[48] Harrington, Dan and Robertie, Bill. (2004). *Harrington on Hold 'em Expert Strategy for No-Limit Tournaments*. (Two Plus Two Publishing).

I'm not going to win this hand, I'm fairly sure I will be able to get you next time." It also shows that a player is patient enough to wait for a better position.

Because each round has different monetary significance, depending on how many chips the players decide to wager, all rounds are not created equal. A player who wins 12 hands worth 10 chips each will fall well behind a player who wins one hand worth 1,000 chips. It's not how many hands you win, it's how many chips you win that matters.

An examiner folds by moving on to a new line of questioning. After failing to secure an admission or deciding that asking more questions on a given issue will not prove productive, the examiner moves on. The witness folds by surrendering an admission instead of using a lawyer's objection, introducing an agenda or waffling. Folding is an important part of cross-examination since the examiner will not win every line of questioning he starts and the witness will occasionally be out of position. Staying with questions that will not bear fruit means wagering more credibility on an unlikely bet. If you are not going to win the hand, why bet more chips?

> *Q: Is a free market economy a competitive economy?*
>
> *A: There are elements of competition and cooperation in a free market economy. It's not entirely one or the other.*
>
> *Q: OK. So is it more competitive or cooperative?*
>
> *A: Again, that's hard to say. Um ... some free market economies display attributes of competition. Others have a cooperative side.*

The judge is thinking, *Why don't you just say "yeah" already?* Each non-response is calling your opponent's bet. The examiner is inviting you to push more credibility into the pot, knowing that the final showdown will have him raking in the chips. The witness is bleeding chips unnecessarily. Stop. Say "sure." When you're backed into a corner, give the examiner what he wants. Another hand follows. There will be other issues to disagree on and you will probably have better position on those topics. Save some credibility chips for then.

Cross-examination is never the last element in a debate round. There will always be an opportunity to resurrect issues and regain lost ground. No hill is worth dying on in cross-examination. Try to bust out your opponent in just one hand and you may end up busting out yourself.

The "I Don't Know" Fold

We discussed the credible deployment of "I don't know" earlier. For the purpose of the poker analogy, if you admit that you are unaware of something you should know, you are folding. Admit your lack of knowledge as soon as it is credibly possible and do not chase the issue with chips. If you misrepresent your knowledge by implying you know something you really don't, you are throwing away chips.

If you are able to credibly admit you do not know the answer (either because the question is unreasonable or you have demonstrated an adequate peripheral understanding of the issue) you split the pot with your opponent. Neither side gains or loses credibility. Consider our earlier example:

> *Q: How many dimples are there on a golf ball?*
>
> *A: I don't know.*

You may be able to actually gain points with an "I don't know." If the examiner asks an outrageously unreasonable question, a confident "I don't know" or short quip may pull credibility away from your opponent.

> *Q: How many dimples are there on a golf ball?*
>
> *A: Wilson or Spalding?*

Because a credible "I don't know" splits the pot, you shouldn't be afraid of it. It is much better to split the pot than to call the examiner's bets a few times before folding.

Fold Confidently

Watch a professional poker player. He looks down at his cards, registering no visible reaction. The cards might be aces or they might by 2-7, we have no way of knowing. If the card player folds, he pushes his cards away. If he is feeling especially gesticular, he may shrug. He never sighs or acts disappointed. He is not tortured by the decision to fold. It is something he does because math requires it.

The key to maintaining credibility while folding is to be confident. Remember that folding is not a defeat. Debaters who grimace while admitting a question, or act flustered and say, "Let's move on," tell the judge they have been defeated. Be the player who folds by calmly flipping his cards into the muck. Admit an issue nonchalantly because another hand follows. Keep your poker face and be confident once you have decided to fold.

Expected Value

If poker's first lesson is to reduce betting on bad hands, the second lesson is how to recognized good hands. There are relatively few truly premium hands, guaranteed winners that should be exploited to the maximum. Somewhere between the nuts and the rags there are playable hands, good enough for betting in some situations but not in others. So how do you decide whether or not to bet?

Poker players rely on the concept of expected value, which defines the relationship between risk and gain. Even in the simplest situation, you need to consider three variables in order to determine the relevant odds: the amount of the raise, the likelihood of success and the size of the pot. For example, if you are holding four cards to an open-ended straight, with one card yet to be dealt, your chance of completing the straight is roughly five to one (17.4%). Assume that there has been a bet to you of 10 chips, and you must decide whether to call or fold. Your willingness to risk 10 chips on a five-to-one shot depends on the payoff—the size of the pot. Only if the pot is larger than 60 chips does the bet have a positive expected value, in which case you should call. Otherwise, it has a negative expectation and you should fold.

Expected value may justify asking a question to which you don't know the answer. Although traditional cross-examination advice is to avoid asking any question to which you do not know the answer, expected value may justify some fishing expeditions. If you feel it is likely that you will get a usable answer out of a question, it may be worth it to ask—as long as you are betting your credibility for value and not gambling it aimlessly!

In the octa-final round at the national tournament, my partner and I were negative against a case we had never heard of before. It dealt with piracy on the eastern coast of Africa, especially around Somalia. The resolution was about trade with Africa, so the case had some relevance. But we marveled at how such an issue could have escaped our research. (Note that Somali pirates have since become a world news staple.) At the table, we speculated that the case must be weak on significance. A substantial problem, we guessed, would have appeared on our research radar. We decided that the expected value of a targeted fishing expedition on significance was worth risking some credibility.

My partner prepared a few lines of questioning about the frequency, severity and scope of the pirate attacks. His cross-examination revealed that at the time, only 15 ships had been taken over in the last 20 years and that the pirates had yet to take anyone's life. His questions unveiled the success of the status quo's anti-piracy measures and garnered several solid admissions on significance. Before the round, we had no idea that the United States and several other NATO countries already had a strong military presence in that theater. After my partner's cross-examination, that became a central theme of our negative advocacy.

The safest way to play, of course, is to avoid asking questions to which you don't know the answer. You don't want to be the player who bets "his liver to see the river," as the old saying goes. Asking a question out of curiosity is the equivalent of hoping to fill your hand on the river. But when the expected value of those questions is high, such queries might be justified. Do some detective work at the table. Try to guess where the case will be the weakest and design questions to target those areas. If you are reasonably sure you'll catch something and there is a big return available, go ahead and ask.

"Do I Have the Best Hand Now?"

When another player raises aggressively after a community card is revealed, a skilled poker player has to wonder whether his hand is still the winner. Cards that started as winners may take an ugly turn when a bad card is revealed. The skilled player is willing to fold out of these losing hands once their disposition is revealed.

This gives us an important insight into cross-examination: Dragging out a line of questioning is unlikely to make it better. If your examination begins badly, it will generally end badly, because a strong witness can rarely be rattled by extended questioning—especially within the time limits imposed by academic forensics. You may be frustrated by the witness's unjustified display of confidence, you might have reasonably expected your initial questions to blow her out of the water, but there is seldom much to be gained by continuing to badger a tough witness.

There is an omnipresent temptation to stick with a promising line of questioning, challenging the witness with preambles like, "Do you really believe ..." and, "Yet you still say ..." But those tactics are usually ineffectual, very much like betting against a stronger hand. Yes, you might sometimes succeed in shaking the witness or getting her to back off, but it is just as likely that the witness will improve her own position by deflecting the repeated jabs.

Ask yourself whether you still hold the premium position. Even if your line of questioning "should have" succeeded, you can only hurt yourself by not acknowledging its shortcoming. If you draw dead, move to a new line.

Silence the Calling Reflex

Rookie poker players love to call. They think the next card will fill their inside straight. They believe that their hand will improve on the river. If you deconstruct a new card player's thought process, you will see him looking for reasons—*inventing* reasons—to call. He wants badly to stay in the hand and keep believing it will improve. Just as poker players learn to suppress this reflex, debaters need to learn to back off when talking no longer serves a productive purpose.

Perhaps no witness ever suffered the impacts of the calling reflex worse than President William Jefferson Clinton. A Yale-educated attorney, Rhodes scholar and consummate politician and debater, Clinton understood the complexity of argumentation better than most. But in the crucible of cross-examination, when brevity could have been the heart of his defense, he could not restrain himself.[49]

---

[49] Linder, Douglas. (2010). Famous Trials. URL: http://www.law.umkc.edu/faculty/projects/ftrials/ftrials.htm ACCESSED: March 17, 2010.

Clinton's moment of truth came on August 17, 1998, when he appeared for questioning before a grand jury empaneled by Special Council Kenneth Starr. The president's lawyers had obviously counseled him that short answers were essential, and at first it seemed that he understood. But it was not long before Clinton started expanding on his responses. Even when questions called for simple "yes" or "no" answers, he would elaborate at length, often adding details that would come back to haunt him. The major faux pas occurred when the prosecutor was pursuing a line of questioning about events in the Paula Jones case. During the president's deposition, his lawyer had asserted that "there is absolutely no sex of any kind in any manner, shape or form, with President Clinton."

> *Q: That statement is a completely false statement. Is that correct?*
>
> *A: It depends on what the meaning of the word "is" is. If the—if he—if "is" means is and never has been, that is not—that is one thing. If it means there is none, that was a completely true statement.*

A simple "yes" would have sufficed. President Clinton knew he was beaten, but insisted on calling the prosecutor's bet—to disastrous consequences. His absurd waffle was replayed *thousands* of times in the national media and became a late-night punch line. All this could have been avoided had the president been willing to fold. Silence the calling reflex.

Raise

When your opponent brings the cross-examination into territory where you are strong, feel free to push more credibility chips into the pot. If you are confident you will win, why not make the hand more expensive for your opponent?

> *[Bet] Q: On your value, you said that the Nash Equilibrium is an example of where cooperation would work better?*
>
> *[Raise] A: Not only would it work better, the Nash Equilibrium is a mathematical proof showing how we can avoid the Prisoner's Dilemma where everyone ends up worse off.*
>
> *[Re-raise] Q: But aren't there times when competition gets a better outcome?*

> *[Re-raise]* *A: Not at all. Whenever you see a Nash Equilibrium, everyone's expected return increases with cooperation. Competition necessarily produces a worse outcome.*

The witness is obviously very confident in his position because his response to the examiner's betting is to raise. These raises highlight a key point of disagreement between the speakers, but also show that the witness is a firm believer in her position. She is willing to put a lot of credibility behind her position and is forcing the examiner to match her bets in order to stay in the round. If you know you are strong—if you know you hold the aces—why not push back? Use the examiner's question as an opportunity to further elucidate your enthusiasm for your position.

Raise to Stay in Control

Poker great Doyle Brunson argues that the best poker strategy is almost always either to fold (when you have nothing) or raise (with good cards). "If you're going to call," he says, "you might as well bet."[50] Brunson's advice is based on the fact that the card player who raises—forcing others in the hand to raise as well—will gain control of the hand. The raiser generally decides how many chips will be bet after each community card is revealed and determines the price for other players to keep playing. The raiser also has two ways to win (at a showdown or by forcing all the other players to fold), while the caller can only win at a showdown.

In cross-examination, it is imperative to assert early control. When things start to go wrong, they tend to keep going wrong. It is far easier to contain a witness's answers early than it is to bring her back under control after she has steered the examination far from your intended target. Once the witness has launched into a series of lengthy, non-responsive answers, it can be costly or even impossible to get back on track. The examiner's efforts to limit off-topic responses—"Answer *yes* or *no*"—may come off as belligerent or badgering, costing you valuable credibility. Worse, you may draw unwanted attention to the witness's

---

50 Brunson, Doyle. (2003). *Doyle Brunson's Super System: A Course in Power Poker.* (Cardoza). p. 503

responses, underscoring their significance and creating the impression that you have something to hide.

Raising means establishing tight control from the outset, even if it does not seem important at the time. Instead of leading with open-ended questions or phrasing queries that allow ample waffle room, establish a pattern of authority. Use yes or no questions. Point out non-responsive answers. Use your first minute as a trendsetting period to establish the tone for the rest of the examination. You may think broad questions will make you friendlier and less confrontational, but it is far less risky to take control from the outset.

The Benefits of Bluffing

Bluffing generally means that you represent with your bets a stronger position than you actually have. The best way to accomplish this in cross-examination is when you are answering questions. A witness who shifts from vigorous obstructionism to voluntary transparency sends a message that he is very confident in his material. This strategy is especially potent with debaters who have developed a reputation as blusterers or who are not often taken seriously because of their regular evasiveness. By becoming suddenly forthright, they can surprise the examiner and build a credible facade.

Game theorists John von Neumann and Oskar Morgenstern, in their classic academic analysis of poker, argue that bluffing is an essential component of optimum strategy because it conveys "confusing information" to the opposition.[51]

Play Solid Positions

The best defense to a bluff is taking a position that you can defend well. Poker players routinely fold mediocre hands when facing a strong opening bet. Because you have some say in what your hand will be—you decide what arguments to run and what case to write—you should only

---

[51] Neumann, John von and Morgenstern, Oskar. (1980). *Theory of Games and Economic Behavior.* (Princeton University Press).

play positions in which you have high confidence. If you like your case and believe in it, a bluff will not push you away.

Take Your Time

Poker players manipulate time for their advantage. They will pause to consider calling a big bet or how to proceed in a high-stakes hand. Sometimes they linger over the math required for expected value and other considerations. Other times they stop to throw off the rhythm of their opponent.

Like poker, cross-examination is an exchange. The examiner cannot reasonably ask his next question until the witness has finished answering (or at least recited the gist of an answer) to the last question. You control this element of the pace of the exchange. Take time as you need it. If you need to consider a question, take a moment to ponder it. Pauses are a perfectly reasonable element of human interaction. Think about how strange conversation would be without them! Be patient and let the game come to you.

Consider the Size of the Pot

Pot size refers to the number of chips in the pot at any given point. If poker players bet and call aggressively, the value of a pot can be bid up rapidly. The danger is that if too much gets put in the pot—if the card players stake too much on the outcome of a single issue—they will not be able to fold. Debaters who allow too much of their credibility to be wagered behind a single issue may find that the judge ties the outcome of the round to that issue.

My brother, Jesse, and his partner debated in a final round at a major regional tournament. His affirmative case dealt with changing the way the Environmental Protection Agency regulates carbon dioxide emissions. Carbon dioxide is a greenhouse gas and there is some debate in the academic and science communities about whether it contributes substantially to global climate change. Through the course of the tournament, Jesse's strong evidence against the link between man-made carbon dioxide and climate change had gained some notoriety. In the semifinal round, for example, the issue was central to the round's ultimate disposition.

The negative debaters in the final round took a different strategy. They decided to skirt altogether the issue of the global warming impacts of carbon dioxide. In the first negative constructive, the negative took no position on this controversial and pivotal subject, inviting the following exchange in cross-examination:

> *[Bet] Q: In your opinion, do man-made carbon dioxide emissions cause global warming?*
>
> *[Raise] A: You know ... I never took a position on that in my speech.*
>
> *[Re-raise] Q: OK. What is the negative team's stance on this issue?*
>
> *[Re-raise] A: The argument I made was, uh, that your figures were not accurate and I said under "Reason for Change 3" that the amount of carbon dioxide in the atmosphere may be small relative to other elements, but that it could be a large amount overall.*
>
> *[Re-raise] Q: Do you believe that man-made carbon dioxide emissions cause global warming?*
>
> *[Raise] A: Again, Jesse, I don't have a view or opinion.*
>
> *[Re-raise] Q: Does the negative team have a position?*
>
> *[Re-raise] A: [Pause] My position was that there are a number of factors that contribute to global warming.*
>
> *[Re-raise] Q: But do carbon dioxide emissions contribute to global warming?*
>
> *[Re-raise] A: I did not take a position in my speech.*

The cross-examination continued in this vein for over a minute and a half. If you're keeping score at home, that's half the period dedicated to a single line of questioning. Both sides refused to budge. The witness never admitted that carbon dioxide emissions don't link to climate change or gave any position on the issue. Jesse would not back off his question. When time expired, there were so many chips on this line of questioning that the judges were all convinced it was an important issue.

The ballots bore out this conclusion: Five of the seven judges mentioned the exchange. Of those five, two thought Jesse should have moved on quicker. Both of those judges voted negative. The other three judges gave

Jesse high marks in cross-examination. One judge even wrote a "10" next to his cross-examination speaker points, even though only five are allowed, and another put "excellent cx" in three places on the ballot. All three of those judges voted affirmative.

Jesse knew strategically that the carbon dioxide hill was worth dying on. He had good evidence on the issue and knew it was integral to his case. He was willing to push in his chips to defend that point. He chose his hand and bet aggressively. The result was a win and a tournament championship.

I am sure that if the negative speaker were to do that cross-examination over again, he would have given a position, effectively calling Jesse's raises and limiting the growth of the pot. He might have even folded.

Don't Lose Chips on a Formality

There are some times in cross-examination when it's very easy to inadvertently throw away your credibility chips. I call these the courtesy formalities. Depending on your judge, you may have to devote more time than normal to personal formalities such as, "How are you doing today?" and, "Thanks, that's all I have for you." When answering your opponent's courtesy formalities, do not be flippant or harsh. Return the respect and decency that is given to you. Say you are doing well, even if you are not. Do not go into detail about a sore between your toes or describe your medical condition the way you would to a triage nurse. Ask and answer the courtesy questions politely and respectfully. Fumbling the formalities means tossing chips into the rubbish pile.

The Poker Face

Common poker advice is that unless you are an expert on human expressions (someone like Dr. Cal Lightman on the TV show *Lie to Me*), you should ignore subtleties in the way players react to their cards. Despite this advice and its forensics corollary, debaters still wonder what it means when the witness's hand starts shaking. Is it a sign of deception or emotion? Is the witness hiding something or merely nervous about the spotlight? Unfortunately, it is impossible to effectively generalize.

Trembling hands or held breath must mean something, but it is likely to be different for every witness.

Even if there is no universal key to a witness's body language, there are a number of commonly held perceptions about demeanor and truthfulness. These insights are useful for debaters to avoid subtle reactions that send the wrong message to the judge. Shaking hands and shifting posture will almost always be interpreted as signs of deceit. Speech patterns that are unnaturally short or clipped, hesitation and stammering, verbal tics, garbled or fragmented language, voice tremors and constant self-reference ("in my opinion") are also seen as signs of falsity.

The witness's attitude is important. Self-righteousness, anger or aggressiveness—even when seemingly justified by circumstances—will often be construed as dishonesty. So will a pronounced lack of emotion or completely flat delivery, so in debate, a perfect poker face is actually a disadvantage. The other most frequently perceived indicators of deceit are rapid blinking, lack of eye contact, stupid grinning, folded arms and overactive hand gestures. Your cross-examination will certainly improve when you correct these things.[52]

Handling Losses

In life, poker and debate, losses are inevitable. How people handle those losses distinguishes true champions. Losing is part of any competitive activity. No one is immune to it and even the most skilled debaters drop a ballot now and then. In the long run, the best speakers will rise to the top. But the short run is more prone to statistical noise and outliers. And the short run is longer than most people know, or at least it can feel that way.

Forget about the last round and concentrate on the next. Outbursts may feel good, but they never accomplish anything positive. Judgment becomes clouded when frustration sets in, and foolish temptations seem somehow irresistible. When the cross-examination is going poorly, keep your cool. Acknowledge the risk of making emotional decisions and keep from doing anything rash.

---

[52] Brunson, Doyle. (2005). *Super System 2: A Course in Power Poker.* (Cardoza Publishing). pp. 167-176.

Poker and Debate Are Not Life

A life strategy based wholly on poker would be a disaster. Poker values deception and the ability to trick your opponent out of his chips. Someone who approached life with this attitude would find it hard to make friends, and impossible to "win." Author (and poker player) Michael Konik says that "in poker, you have to lie to win; in life telling lies will only make you lose."[53] So the final lesson from poker is that it is *only* a game. It is a controlled experiment in human psychology, game theory and statistics. When you lose at poker, life goes on. When you lose at debate, know that it is preparing you for life outside competition, not the other way around.

* * * * *

Although I am aware of no text (beyond this one) that connects poker to academic debate, I have found several books that discuss it in the context of courtroom argumentation. If you're interested, read Steven Lubet's 2006 Oxford University Press book called *Lawyer's Poker: 52 Lessons That Lawyers Can Learn From Card Players*. Also check out Mark Herrmann's *The Curmudgeon's Guide to Practicing Law,* from American Bar Association. For poker strategies generally, read Alan N. Shoonmaker's *The Psychology of Poker,* from Two Plus Two Publishing. For less academic insights, check out Gus Hansen's *Every Hand Revealed,* a 2008 book from Citadel.

---

[53] Konik, Michael. (2001). *Telling Lies and Getting Paid.* (Huntington Press).

Students who attain excellent CX skills become championship debaters

CHAPTER 7

Cross-Examination Drills

"Pardon me, sir," said a young man, a newcomer to New York, walking up to an elderly gentleman. "Can you tell me how to get to Carnegie Hall?"

"Practice."

I'm targeting coaches in this chapter. Anyone who wants to improve their debate skills can read and try these drills on their own, but the directions are written with a coach in mind.

The drills work best in small groups of no more than 8-10 participants. Use them to break the ice, to increase a class's energy level or to help students practice a particular skill. Delivery is best improved through repetition and example. Drills allow debaters to "feel" their way through a new skill or methodology until it becomes imprinted, like muscle memory. They allow speakers to overcome fears, become more confident in their delivery and warm up before tournaments.

If you discover a compelling variant or "house rule," feel free to modify the instructions indicated here. These drills are just a starting point. Make them fit your club and your students' personalities. To make the drills effective, first explain to students the purpose and objective of each one. Give explicit, detailed instructions—even a mini-lecture on the skill being taught. Be patient with participants who need more time. Provide gentle correction where needed, but always strive to create a non-threatening, fun atmosphere.

Piranha Pack

Purpose: To practice delivering and receiving lines of questions and to explore cases for their cross-examination weaknesses. This drill is responsible for the vast majority of improvement in cases in our club. Early affirmative drafts are guided and molded based on questions that are raised in Piranha Pack.

Instructions: Ask for a student volunteer to read his or her case in front of the club. The case can be either affirmative or negative, but should be complete. Have the others listen and prepare cross-examination questions. When the speech is complete, invite each participant to present one line of questions. Unless you feel time is being abused, impose no limit on the examinations. Everyone should be able to keep asking questions until no one has any more.

Where it is not apparent, ask students why they chose the questions they did. Evaluate responses as a class and ask the students if they can improve the case to remedy weaknesses revealed by the group examination. Piranha Pack makes a great way to lead into a class case discussion or to isolate particular problems in cross-examination. If a student makes a consistent mistake, it will also be apparent during the Piranha Pack. Take time to identify errors to truly make the Piranha Pack a learning experience.

Journalist's Questions

Purpose: To get students thinking in questions and teach participants how to quickly think of simple, short questions.

Instructions: Stand in the front of the room and have participants ask a series of questions to elicit a description of your clothing. Each participant, in turn, must ask a question with Who, What, When, Where, Why, Describe, Explain, etc., as the preface, using one short sentence, preferably 15 words or less. As the participants start to figure out the drill, have them use fewer words—10 words or less, then eight words and so on. Assign a student to police the word count and eliminate those who cannot quickly think of a question that fits the criteria. The drill ends when one student is left.

Picture Perfect

Purpose: To get students thinking in questions and to teach participants how to think of simple, short questions.

Instructions: Ask each participant to draw a picture of something. Have them pair up and describe their pictures to each other. Next, ask all of the pairs to stand up. Have one member of each pair lead the other through an examination of his or her picture. Only the student playing the role of the witness should be able to see the picture. The goal is to use questions to clarify the drawing so that the student acting as the examiner can identify the image without looking at the picture. Then have the participants change roles, with the other member of the pair conducting the examination. The whole room will be filled with noise as the participants learn to describe a series of marks on a paper to lead their partner to the conclusion about what object was drawn.

Freeze-Frame: The Pen

Purpose: Although life moves quickly, it can be thought of as a series of frames, strung together like images in a video. Debaters rarely ask cross-examination questions about personal events, but doing so is important for developing the ability to come up with good questions in a debate round. This drill will hone participants' ability to use the "freeze-frame" approach to develop a point, emphasize it and make its importance apparent to the judge.

Instructions: Have a student stand in front of the class, reach into his pocket, withdraw a pen, and drop it on the ground. Advise the participants to watch the student closely. Then direct them to cross-examine on the act they have just observed. Have the participants ask a minimum of 10 questions, making a relatively quick act seem like a long process. A single leading question like, "Did you drop your pen?" is not the aim. Rather, examiners should be encouraged to start small and stay small ("Was your hand at your side? Did you begin to lift it? Did you lift it to chest level? Did you put your hand inside your pocket?"). Have students loop, peg and prod with their questions. Ask for another volunteer to drop another object to continue the exercise.

Variant: After the student drops the pen, tell the questioners that instead of a pen, a bomb was dropped. Have them conduct the freeze-frame cross-examination as before, but allow them to include questions about the pen-dropping student's feelings and emotions ("Were you scared? Were you shaking?").

Variant: Do the Pen Drill, above, but permit each participant to ask only three or four questions and then name another participant to continue the drill.

Group Tree

Purpose: To develop cross-examination routines and build effective routines as a club.

Instructions: Distribute a copy of an affirmative or negative position to all participants or have a student read the case aloud. Tell the students that you are going to create a great cross-examination routine as a group. Begin the brainstorming by writing the desired final admission on the board. Ask students to shout out possible questions. For each query write down the possible answers and develop follow-up questions. The drill is concluded when an effective routine has been created. Repeat as necessary to develop a complete cross-examination strategy against a particular affirmative or negative.

Theme

Purpose: To practice incorporating key thematic terms into questions.

Instructions: Have a student present a negative argument against another student's case in a Piranha Pack. Invite the student running the affirmative to cross-examine. For this drill, however, write a few key words related to the affirmative's theme (*Accountability* or *Cost-Effectiveness*, for instance) on the board. Tell the examiner that he must incorporate these themes into his questions.

Tennis Ball

Purpose: To focus on the cross-examination instead of concentrating exclusively on notes. Examiners also learn the importance of asking tightly worded queries and avoiding open-ended questions.

Instructions: Conduct a Piranha Pack. Explain to the participants that the only time words can be exchanged in the drill is when someone is holding a tennis ball. Give the ball to the first examiner to lead off the questions. After each question is asked, the examiner is to toss the ball to the witness. The witness then answers the question. Anytime the examiner diverts her eyes from the witness by looking away or at notes, the witness is authorized to throw the tennis ball at the examiner. (Participants should be cautioned against throwing the ball toward the examiner's face or other sensitive areas.) When the examiner finishes answering each question, the tennis ball is tossed back to the examiner. After a participant runs through his questions, he hands the ball to the next examiner.

Conga Line

Purpose: To learn to stay involved in the cross-examination and to think one question ahead.

Instructions: Distribute or have a student read a case as in a Piranha Pack. Have a participant ask a question. As soon as that question is asked, the next student takes control of the cross-examination as the examiner. The exchanges continue, with each student asking one question before passing the reins on to the next student, until the examination is concluded.

Argument Deconstruction

Purpose: To deconstruct arguments and quickly convert positions into their syllogistic form.

Instructions: Print out several news articles, debate cases or policy briefs. (Use a resource like Google News to locate and print out news articles, or visit your favorite think tank for a policy comment.) Distribute one article, case or brief per student and ask participants to read through their article and identify all the arguments they can find. (Arguments will be more apparent in the policy briefs and debate cases, but they are still present in news articles.) Go around the room and ask each student to present the arguments they found in their document in syllogistic form (major premise, minor premise, conclusion).

ACKNOWLEDGEMENTS

No project of this size can be undertaken without significant support and assistance. While I can't possibly thank everyone who helped along this text, I extend my sincere gratitude to the following—

Joel and Martine Herche. You listened to, advised, nurtured, encouraged and admonished your ambitious son. You still do. Every accomplishment in my life owes itself in some measure to your contributions. Thank you!

Mike and Mary Winther. You taught me how to debate and guided my youthful enthusiasm. You are two of the best debate coaches I have ever met.

Mark Bowman. You taught me my first lessons in cross-examination and many more after that.

Parents of Envoy Speech and Debate. Your valuable feedback and criticism helped eliminate zany strategies and bring the best ones to light.

My students. Your motivation and enthusiasm fuels mine. Thanks for letting me live my love of forensics vicariously through you.

Chris Jeub. We share a wonderful vision to train minds for action. It's been a pleasure working with you on this important work.

Steve Isaacs. Behind every good writer is a great editor. You are a great editor. This product is but one more piece of evidence in support of that fact.

Jesse Byrnes. Thanks for the layout and editing work. Your discipline under deadline will serve you well.

My Creator. This is all for you.

ABOUT THE AUTHOR

Cody Herche

Cody was the team debate high school national champion in 2006 and the top Lincoln-Douglas speaker in 2005. He still holds the record for individual speaker points set at the 2004 Worlds Parliamentary Tournament with 296 out of a possible 300 points. Herche has taught at camps and conferences around the country and instructed numerous state and national qualifiers, finalists and champions, including the 2007 team policy champions and 2010 Lincoln-Douglas champion. He is the author of *Keys to Extemp* and edits *Gold Book: The current events sourcebook*.

Elected into *Phi Beta Kappa* as a junior, Herche graduated *Summa Cum Laude* in economics from the University of the Pacific. He is currently a J.D. candidate at Cornell Law School in New York.